Advance Praise for *Vegetarian Comfort Foods*

"This book will make your gut giddy with joy! Jennifer's easy-to-read information, practical advice, delicious healthy recipes, and meal plans make it so easy to improve your digestion and reclaim your health."

—Tess Masters, author of *The Blender Girl* cookbook

"What we eat affects our bodies, and by being mindful about what we nourish ourselves with, we make progress towards improved health and a better life. Browne's *Vegetarian Comfort Foods* encourages clean and fun food, and overall better nutrition choices."

—Jared Koch, founder & CEO of Clean Plates

"Many of us would love to improve our diets and take control of our health—but where to start? In *Vegetarian Comfort Foods*, Jennifer Browne makes it fun, tasty, and eminently doable with a fabulous collection of healthful recipes. Combining solid nutrition facts with personal anecdotes and delicious food, it's as inspiring as it is practical."

—Kim Foster, MD, family physician, author, and health blogger.

"As an athletic, happy vegan for over twenty years, I believed that my diet was optimal, and that it provided the necessary fuel and support to keep me experiencing an active, high-achieving lifestyle. And then along came Jennifer's *Happy Healthy Gut* and *Vegetarian Comfort Foods*, and my 'best self' was surpassed! I am grateful to Jennifer for writing easy-to-understand, fun, and enjoyable books that not only educate me further on my own body, but have brought me to greater understanding of how to improve my beloved plant-based diet and improve my digestion simultaneously. Let's Eat!"

—Bif Naked, international recording artist, activist, vegan

"In this day of constant bombardment of junk food, it's refreshing to come across a recipe book that is designed to teach us how to eat for good digestive health. *Vegetarian Comfort Foods* is not only a book that's easy to read and follow, it has an abundance of simple, easy recipes to get you there quickly."

—Sylvia Tarnuzzer, nutrition and weight-loss coach

Vegetarian Comfort Foods

The Happy Healthy Gut Guide to Delicious
Plant-Based Cooking

VEGETARIAN COMFORT FOODS

JENNIFER BROWNE

Skyhorse Publishing

Skyhorse Publishing books may be purchased in bulk at special discounts for sales promotion, corporate gifts, fund-raising, or educational purposes. Special editions can also be created to specifications. For details, contact the Special Sales Department, Skyhorse Publishing, 307 West 36th Street, 11th Floor, New York, NY 10018 or info@skyhorsepublishing.com.

Skyhorse® and Skyhorse Publishing® are registered trademarks of Skyhorse Publishing, Inc.®, a Delaware corporation.

Visit our website at www.skyhorsepublishing.com.

10 9 8 7 6 5 4 3 2 1

Library of Congress Cataloging-in-Publication Data is available on file.

Cover design by Anna Christian
Cover photo by Wild Honey Art House

Print ISBN: 978-1-63220-332-8
Ebook ISBN: 978-1-63220-747-0

Printed in China

Acknowledgments

A project such as this one cannot be completed by only one person. Turns out, it takes a lot of enthusiastic believers (and many hungry mouths, willing to taste a lot of food!) to create a cookbook.

Thank you to Skyhorse Publishing for giving me the incredible opportunity to express my excitement for plant-based eats in this book. I believe that food is everything. Just as it contributes to health, strength, and survival, it is also responsible for sickness, weakness, and disease. Understanding how food works with your body and choosing to use that knowledge for the purpose of growth and repair is one of the most important things you can do for yourself. I'm genuinely blessed to have been given the chance to inspire others to create new and nourishing dishes for themselves and their families.

Thanks to my generous friends, Andreas and Marlene, for lending us their beautiful kitchen to shoot in, and to Tanya R. Loewen of Wild Honey Art House, who photographed my favorite foods and made them look much prettier than I ever could.

To those who lent us fabulous dishes and backdrops for many of the recipes— Gary, Joy, Judy, Kory, and Tanya—I can't thank you all enough!

Finally, a shout-out to the lovely few who contributed recipes: Andreas, Karley, Marie, and Natalie. Thanks so much for sharing! This book is better because of you.

Lastly, to Seventh Avenue Literary—I am grateful.

Dedication

For those who have inspired me to live a better life—the amazing people who have shouted to the rooftops that food is the best medicine, that the body is self-healing, and that being mindful about what goes into your mouth is a necessity for living happily and healthfully. I was listening, and others are too.

For my children, whom I hope are growing up to understand what real food is, and why that's important.

Lastly, for Dave, for letting me get away with my ridiculous ideas, not calling me out on my compulsiveness, eating every last bit of anything I put in front of him, and *never* bursting my bubbles.

Contents

On Being Mindful about What You Eat

"Homicide is 0.8% of deaths. Diet-related disease is over 60%. But no one f***ing talks about it."[1] —Jamie Oliver

I truly believe that food nourishes your entire body and soul, and that to be healthy and happy, you need to adopt the mindset that food is fuel. Nothing is more important than your body's ability to grow and repair, and the food we choose to eat is directly related to how well we can accomplish this.

A few years ago, I had been sick for nearly a decade with irritable bowel syndrome (IBS). You know what healed my body and eradicated my symptoms? You guessed it—food. Good food. Whole, plant-based, mindfully-chosen food. That's it! If food could help me get healthy, then food can help you, too. For this reason, I'm thrilled to be able to share with you the kind of food that my body (and *your* body) craves. You might not know it yet, but somewhere in that beautiful body of yours, your cells are begging for the type of nourishment that the recipes in this book can provide.

When I began my journey to improved health and wellbeing

(Digestive Bliss Town is actually what I called it in my first book, *Happy Healthy Gut: The Natural Diet Solution to Curing IBS and Other Chronic Digestive Disorders*), I needed all the help I could get. For this reason, I've included some information on pantry prerequisites, kitchen tools, cleansing, and a few other goodies. But the largest portion of this book is dedicated to my favorite recipes, divided into nine different categories of food: Juice, Smoothies, Sauces & Dressings, Wake & Break, Nibbles, Sides, Rawsome Salads, Main Eats, and delicious Sweet Tooth must-haves. They are all whole and plant-based, meaning that 95 percent of the ingredients derive from a plant source. Each and every recipe is vegetarian, most are full-on vegan, and the majority are gluten-free, too. For those of you who abstain from any and all animal products, I offer substitutions on a per-recipe basis to get you there, if the recipe isn't there already. Don't worry—I have your back!

If you've read *Happy Healthy Gut* and wished for more tummy-taming recipes, this book is for you. As someone who has talked the talk and walked the walk where digestive disease and recovery are concerned, I want you to know that these recipes are what got me to where I am today: happy, healthy, and IBS-free. (Hallelujah!) Even if you don't have trouble with digestion, the foods included in this book can only make your body feel better, and become noticeably more nourished. This is because all of the recipes are easy for your body to process, and contain high levels of nutrients for your intestinal tract to absorb.

Here's why you should read this book: we are all capable of being as healthy as we want to be, and if you find that "healthy" is not an adjective you would use to describe yourself, let me show you how to get there. If you're already there (good for you!), then this book will remind you of a few things you've likely forgotten, and hopefully fill you in on areas you may be confused about. As long as we continue to ask questions about our foodstuffs, incorporate new foods into our diet, listen to our bodies, and be truly kind to ourselves, health and happiness will follow with every single delicious bite.

My Thoughts on Consuming Animal Products

This topic is a toughie, and I'll begin by disclosing that I do occasionally eat them in the forms of sustainable seafood, free-range eggs, and organic dairy. I think what one chooses to eat is a very personal choice, and that no one should be berated or made to feel inferior for choosing a lifestyle that is different from someone else's. That being said, those of us suffering from health issues that could be absolved by tweaking our diet should definitely consider doing so. Giving up animal products (even temporarily so that you can see the difference it makes to your body) is *beyond* worth it if you're experiencing chronic illness. It's also free and carries no ill side effects, unlike prescription medications and unnecessary surgeries. I know this, because I experienced the amazing effects of doing this myself, several years ago.

I originally cut items like poultry, beef, and pork from my diet—because of health reasons—in 2010. I just couldn't digest those foods, so I chose to remove them in order to reap the rewards that come along with a healthy digestive system (a.k.a. bowel regularity). While researching my decision I learned a lot, including the fact that animal products are acidic and can change the pH of your body to the point that disease flourishes. I also found out that they are very high in saturated fat and contribute greatly to coronary heart disease, cancer, obesity, and other chronic health issues.

But one of the biggest eye-openers for me was the fact that the production of conventional animal products are completely environmentally unsustainable, and that food animals are typically incredibly mistreated. Although the decision to exclude the majority of animal products from my diet had originally been to create a smoother digestive experience, it evolved to become a conscious decision to try and be as healthy as possible, while contributing far less to some of the issues I mentioned above.

So here's what I think: nibble on a piece of fabulously aged cheese every now and then, enjoy the fresh, wild salmon your friend's husband caught while fishing last week, and splurge on a full-fat Starbucks latte every once in awhile. Support local farmers, and be aware of the quality of the products you choose to consume. It doesn't have to be black and white, but you'll feel the most at peace if the grey area in which you choose to reside is lived in mindfully. If you care about your health, then it's your own responsibility to become aware of where your food comes from, what it contains, and how it benefits you. As you become more intimate with what nourishes you, you will begin to unlock the door to a whole new world of health and happiness—one that's been there all along.

The Bottom Line

What this book intends to do is arm you with foods that are designed to make you glow from the inside out. Let it remind you that there are endless possibilities when it comes to cooking, and be your go-to when you need some inspiration. You know what happens when you decide to eliminate a few crappy foods from your diet? You discover incredible new ones that take their place. These recipes are compiled of delicious, colorful, wholesome, plant-based ingredients that are kind to your body and to the environment. To make it super simple, each recipe indicates whether it is vegetarian (v), vegan (V), and/or gluten-free (GF). Because I totally understand the need to indulge, I occasionally include ingredients such as goat cheese to accompany a salad—but like I explained earlier, there are substitutions that are offered if you'd like your meals to remain completely vegan.

I was super-psyched to have the privilege of writing this book. I love good food, I love food photographs, and I love having my food photographed. I hope you enjoy this collection as much as I enjoyed creating it. Thank you so much for giving me the chance to share what I love with you.

Bon appétit!

The Happy Healthy Pantry

"The responsibility to be healthy is in your hands—no one else is going to do it for you."[2] –Cameron Diaz, *The Body Book*

In this section I get to take all of my very favorite ingredients and foods that I cook with and eat on a consistent basis and tell you all about them. What fun! It's no secret that I love food. Even before I began eating for my digestive disorder, I was a total foodie. I've *never* been a picky eater. In fact, the only things I've ever had a hard time with happen to be meat products! My family will attest to the fact that organ meats, clams, frog's legs, and raw meats (such as beef tartare) are really the only things I've ever balked at in the past. And now, since I don't eat that stuff anyway, I haven't come across anything plant-based I would hesitate to shove in my mouth. (And I mean *shove*. That Pistachio Stuffed Figs recipe on page 89? Those are one-biters for this girl.)

The following ingredients are my plant-based mainstays that I cook with throughout this book, but that

doesn't mean that I don't use organic butter and free-range eggs from time to time. I'm not advising that you throw those items out or don't use them—I just recommend you check out some new fun alternatives, try to mix it up, and attempt to step outside your Crisco comfort zone. (But honestly, if you're still using shortening, please stop.) If you're not into milk and egg and cheese substitutions, then that's okay. Food is personal, and cooking should be fun.

If you haven't already, be prepared to fall in love with some new and literally life-changing foods. This is so exciting! Here are my absolute mainstays that make up the largest portions of my pantry, refrigerator, and freezer:

Vegetables & Roots

This category is the absolute center of a plant-based diet. We should all be consuming mostly vegetables throughout the day, because they come with built-in fiber, vitamins, minerals (especially the roots!), and antioxidants. Plants like these create their own defense team against free-radicals, and when we eat them, we strengthen our immune system, improve digestion, and absorb a plenitude of nutrients that keep us healthy and strong. Go, plants!

- Beets
- Bell peppers
- Cabbage (purple)
- Carrots
- Celery
- Corn (organic)
- Cucumbers
- Eggplant
- Endive
- Fennel
- Garlic
- Kale
- Leaf lettuce
- Onions
- Rhubarb
- Romaine lettuce
- Spinach
- Squash (acorn or spaghetti)
- Sweet potatoes
- Swiss chard
- Tomatoes
- Yams
- Zucchini

Fruit

Just like vegetables, fruit is full of the good stuff. It contains more naturally-occurring sugar than veggies do, so one or two pieces of fruit per day is the perfect amount to keep your body nourished, while satisfying your sweet tooth. Whole fruits, like the ones listed below, are a tidy package of fiber, vitamins, and antioxidants. They are much better for your body than processed versions, because when food goes through processing, nutrients are removed, and sugar is added. For example, when you drink store-bought juice, it's not even close to being equal to eating an apple. You miss out on fiber (which helps slow sugar absorption), and the raw enzymes that your body needs and loves. Store-bought juice is dead juice. We want to live, right? Eat fresh and whole—not processed.

- Apples
- Avocado
- Bananas
- Berries (all kinds)
- Cantaloupe
- Dates
- Figs
- Grapefruit
- Grapes
- Kiwi
- Lemons
- Limes
- Oranges
- Pears
- Watermelon

Beans & Legumes

Although there are many varieties that fall into this category, the ones I've listed below are my staples—the ones I have on hand *always*. They're all very different, and super versatile. If you don't prioritize beans and legumes yet, get ready to jump on the Bean Bandwagon. They're full of fiber and protein, and when you're eating primarily vegetarian, they become a huge part of your cooking on a daily basis.

- Black beans
- Garbanzo beans (chickpeas)
- Green beans
- Kidney beans
- Lentils (all colors)
- Sprouted *anything*

Grains

Grains are important. They are the broom of your intestine, and aside from assisting with fabulous digestive health, whole grains provide complex carbohydrates that keep your body awake and your mind alert. They contain the perfect amount of glucose (which is the *only* thing that feeds your brain), and it's released much more slowly than simple sugars are, which tease you with a feel-good high but result in a subsequent crash. Complex carbs—the kind found in whole grains—don't cause that dramatic sugar wreckage, and instead, allow you to stay energized all day long.

The following grains are my favorites, and I cook with at least one of them every day. They contain fiber to bulk up your stool, and can make a boring salad incredible! (Even though it's actually a seed, I'm including quinoa here, because I use it as a grain. Quinoa is actually extra-special, because it's also a complete protein!) If you are trying to remain gluten-free, then it's important to source out gluten-free oats—they can become contaminated with wheat if the crops are grown close to one another.

- Bran germ
- Oats (rolled)
- Quinoa
- Rice (sprouted, brown, wild)

Nuts & Seeds

These suckers are tiny powerhouses that contain good fat, great flavor, and a punch of protein. They make a perfect condiment for salads, and dress up a plain old banana like nobody's business. Chia seeds, in particular, are a complete protein (just like quinoa!) and make a fabulous binder in place of an egg, for all you vegan folks out there. I'm totally nuts for nuts and seeds.

- Almonds
- Cashews
- Chia seeds
- Flax seeds
- Hemp hearts
- Pecans
- Pumpkin seeds
- Pine nuts
- Pistachios
- Sesame seeds
- Sunflower seeds
- Walnuts

Herbs & Spices

Those who insist that vegetarian fare is flavorless obviously haven't tasted it done right. The secret to great cooking is using a fabulous variety of herbs and spices, and the following list outlines what I typically have on hand 24/7. I grow most of the fresh stuff in my garden and buy the rest at farmer's markets, or scoop it from bulk bins if it's dried. If you've never made the effort to cook with herbs and spices, get ready to throw on your party pants (or party apron) and get excited!

Fresh

- Basil
- Cilantro
- Dill
- Garlic
- Ginger
- Mint
- Parsley, Italian flat-leafed
- Parsley, regular

Dried

- Cardamom
- Chili powder
- Cinnamon
- Cumin
- Garlic salt
- Onion powder
- Paprika
- Pepper (black)
- Pepper (cayenne)
- Red pepper flakes
- Sea salt
- Turmeric

*Note: if you have a gluten allergy (celiac disease), you should never buy from bulk bins—they are easily cross-contaminated.

Dairy Alternatives

Although I'm personally not completely vegan, I eat like I am most of the time. Since there are amazing alternatives available, I don't feel like I'm missing out *at all*. With regards to soy, make sure you purchase organic products. Most soy is genetically modified, so that organic label is important in order to avoid GMOs. The following list is comprised of my dairy-free mainstays. If you haven't fallen in love with them already, be prepared to do just that.

- Almond milk
- Coconut milk
- Daiya "cheese"
- Earth's Balance
- Buttery Spread
- Soy milk (organic)
- Soy yogurt (organic)

Sweeteners

I love the following sweeteners so much more than I ever loved refined, white sugar. Most of the sweeteners below are much lower on the Glycemic Index (GI) than refined sugar, and they're also less processed. They all have slightly different flavors, so which one you use will depend on what you're making. I bake a lot with molasses, cane sugar, coconut sugar, and dates. I use the rest for drizzling on my kids' oatmeal or pancakes or adding to homemade frozen treat recipes. Just play around, and you'll get familiar with their strengths.

- Agave syrup
- Black strap molasses
- Brown rice syrup
- Cane sugar (raw)
- Coconut sugar
- Dates (Medjool)
- Honey
- Maple syrup (100% pure)

Oils

Although I typically side-step oil in my baking (I almost always substitute applesauce for oil), it's still sometimes a necessity when it comes to cooking. Yes, you can stir-fry in water. Yes, oil is very high in saturated fat. But you know what? As long as you're only using a little good-quality oil here and there, it won't hurt you. The secret to cooking with oil is figuring out which one will compliment your cooking technique, depending on what you're making. The oils I've listed below are the ones I use all the time, and I've indicated beside them whether they're good for drizzling on salad (no heat), warming (low heat), cooking (medium heat), or stir-frying (high heat). Also, each type of oil has its own flavor, so keep that in mind. (I wouldn't recommend baking banana bread with peanut oil or drizzling melted coconut oil on your salad.)

- Avocado (high heat)
- Coconut (medium/high heat)
- Grape Seed (high heat)
- Flax (no/low heat)
- Olive (no/medium heat)
- Peanut (medium/high heat)
- Safflower (no/low heat)
- Sesame (medium/high heat)

Vinegars

As with oils, acids are to be used in small doses, and each one has its own distinct flavor. Sometimes you can find a lovely vinegar at a farmer's market, and it's fun to mix, match, and experiment. The list of acids below are the ones I use all the time. (Check out the salad dressings on page 57.)

- Balsamic
- Red wine
- Rice
- White
- White wine

Other

I needed to include this last section, because there are more ingredients that don't fall into the categories above that I cook and bake with all the time. They're just as much part of my pantry, and deserve to be given proper acknowledgment. Many of the recipes used in this book refer to the ingredients below, so make sure to check them out.

For Baking:

- **Almond butter.** Gives baking a great consistency and offers protein and fiber. It's a really fantastic alternative to peanut butter, because unless organic, peanuts are typically highly sprayed with chemicals. Other substitutes that I use are sunflower, cashew, pea, and sesame butters.
- **Aluminum-free baking powder.** Why buy the stuff with metal in it if you can buy stuff without?

- **Applesauce**. Unsweetened applesauce has almost completely replaced butter, lard, shortening, eggs, and anything else of this nature in my baking. It's fairly seamless (although breads do come out a little denser), low in fat, and way healthier than the conventional alternatives. Other great substitutes for butter and eggs are pumpkin puree and avocado.
- **Carob chips and cacao nibs**. These are vegan. You can buy these sweetened or un-sweetened, and sub them in for regular chocolate chips. A word to the wise: my kids are not giant fans of the unsweetened version. They're definitely not sweet. (Just sayin'.)
- ***Parchment paper**. I realize that this is not a food (hence the asterisk), but because I don't usually like to use things like oil and butter to coat baking pans, I use a lot of parchment paper. Just make sure you have some handy.
- **All-purpose gluten-free flour**. For those with celiac disease or sensitivity to wheat, this flour is a life saver. Although not usually entirely whole grain, it's still a fabulous substitute for conventional flour, when gluten is a concern.
- **Whole wheat flour** (and other flour substitutes). For those of us who don't need to worry as much about gluten, whole wheat flour is still my favorite. If you *do* have to worry about gluten, then buckwheat flour is a great substitute.

For Cooking:
- **Coconut milk**. I buy the full-fat, canned version of this. It looks solid when you open it, but when you mix it up, it becomes creamy. It offers delicious consistency to stews, soups, and curries. Note: the low-fat version is just not the same. If something is advertised as "low-fat," it's probably been processed more. Just buy full-fat—it tastes better.
- **Miso paste and stock (organic)**. Miso is fermented soy. I use the paste to make dips for wraps and other things, and the stock to make miso soup. Miso has live enzymes in it that are great for digestion.
- **Mustard**. This is one prepared sauce that I would have a very hard time giving up—not that I have to. Mustard is low-fat, tummy-friendly, and comes in different varieties. Search for preparations that are low in ingredients, and use for sandwiches, wraps, salad dressings, and more.

- **Nori**. Dried nori is a life-saver for un-inspired days. Quickly vamp up rice and fresh veggies by rehydrating the seaweed (which is full of all things awesome for you), and roll up whatever you want. Dip in wasabi, and voila! A quick and yummy creation.
- **Nutritional yeast**. This stuff has a cheesy, nutty flavor, so it's great to use as a natural flavor enhancer. It contains live enzymes, and I recommend you buy it fortified with Vitamin B12. I use it in sauces, and sprinkle it on anything from Kale Chips (page 96) to Easy as (Pizza) Pie (page 148). The Red Star brand is my favorite.
- **Refried beans**. Like conventional beans, refried beans are super low in fat, and high in taste and fiber. Place in a grainy wrap with some sprouted brown rice, veggies, and salsa for a quick and healthy veggie burrito.
- **Rice papers**. Like nori, rice papers can make a creative concoction out of plain ingredients. Unlike nori, it does not possess the same nutrient profile. (Nori has one; rice papers don't.) But these suckers are convenient and have a much milder taste for those who haven't yet made the leap to seaweed.
- **Tahini**. Tahini is sesame seed paste, and is a fabulous ingredient for wraps, salad dressings, and all things saucy. I definitely recommend you give it a try.
- **Tamari**. This soy sauce is gluten-free, usually low-salt, and typically organic. It's less processed, and more delicious. I use it for marinades, salad dressings, veggie sauces, and more. Get familiar with this—it's good stuff.
- **Tofu**. Because this is a soy product, it's important that it's organic. Once that hurdle is cleared, the versatility of tofu can be appreciated. I usually use extra-firm, but in reality, different textures can be cooked in different ways. I just happen to like very firm tofu; I use it to make anything from Breakfast Rancheros (page 80) to vegan Tzatziki (page 68).
- **Vegetable soups**. I totally stock cans of vegetable soups in my pantry. Try and get Bisphenol A (BPA) free cans if you can—Eden brand is great. They're awesome for a quick lunch (kind of like a healthy fast-food), and my daughter loves them. Because of the BPA situation, if you can buy pre-made soup in tetra packs, then do that.

- **Vegetable stock**. You can make your own, but I'm not going to lie and say I usually do—I don't. I buy tetra packs of organic vegetable soup stock and bust them out of the pantry on an as-needed basis. I use them to make my own vegetable-lentil soup, as a marinade, or as a buffer between my crockpot and the veggies that are simmering inside of it.
- **Wasabi**. Some people think that eating plant-based means eating flavorless, but that's ridiculous. Wasabi is *amazing*. I love heat, and I love it on everything. I use wasabi traditionally, on veggie rolls, but also as a condiment for sandwiches, veggie burgers, etc. I love the burn—and it's a really good one.
- **Worcestershire sauce**—the vegan kind (no fishy stuff). I can't make my Lazy Cabbage Roll Casserole (page 149) without this, so it made the cut. I love this sauce, and it's great for stir-fries, too. Worcestershire plus tamari equals yumminess. This combo is also featured in the recipe for Eastern Lettuce Wraps (page 159).

Ingredient Substitutions

Before we move on to the next section of this book, I have one more topic to discuss with you: subs. (Ingredient subs, that is.) While some of us have no problem baking with butter, or frying up an egg, a lot of us prefer to completely abstain from animal products all together. This is where the substitutions come in handy.

- **Eggs**. Mixing one tablespoon of ground flaxseed to three tablespoons of water is a great substitute for one egg. Stir until the mixture becomes gelatinous, and you have a perfectly plant-based binder. Also, one egg equals ¼ cup of pureed fruit or soy yogurt. (Something thick and wet and gloppy.) So, instead of using 2 eggs, you could use ½ cup of applesauce, ½ cup of mashed banana, ½ cup canned pumpkin puree, or ½ cup of so yogurt . . . see where I'm going with this?
- **Butter/Lard**. Substitute straight across for applesauce. Instead of ½ cup of butter, use ½ cup of unsweetened applesauce. It works beautifully. Your banana bread will be a little denser, but

who cares? You traded lard in for applesauce. You're magic! This is magic bread.

- **Wheat flour**. Those with celiac disease need not fret—there is gluten-free flour available. The trick is making sure there's xanthan gum in there.
- **Milk**. Use unsweetened organic soy or almond milk if the texture doesn't matter. If it does, and you need something thicker, then use full-fat coconut milk.
- **Cheese**. Some of the recipes in this book use cheese, but you can easily substitute Daiya for it; especially on things like pizza and quesadillas. I'm not a giant fan of soy cheese, but Daiya isn't soy, and it's yummy when you need it.

* If you're substituting both eggs and butter, try and use the flaxseed fix in place of an egg, and the applesauce in place of butter. (Too much fruit puree will make pretty dense bread.)

Fabulously Convenient Kitchen Tools

"A man too busy to take care of his health is like a mechanic too busy to take care of his tools."[3] —Spanish Proverb

Here's my philosophy: why make things harder than they have to be? When it comes to cooking, which we typically engage in at least a couple times a day, *every day*, the investment in a great blender or chef's knife or cast iron skillet *will* be a good one. If cooking becomes more enjoyable for you because of these items, then I say that's good for your whole family, because their food (and yours!) will be created with love and fun instead of boredom and frustration.

The following tools are ones I use on a weekly, or sometimes daily, basis. I've sworn up and down that onions will never again make me cry (thank you, food processor), and salsa will never take me twenty-five minutes to whip up. Dry eyes and a five to ten minute investment, tops— that's what I'm talking about. Here's my top ten, personal list of must-haves for the Plant-Based Kitchen Goddess:

Food processor. A food processor makes life easier when learning how to prepare your own food from scratch for two reasons: it's faster, and it makes cooking fun. Adopting the concept of "whole food" really means preparing everything yourself. You can cut corners here and there (I certainly do), but for the most part, you're doing things like making your own salsa, pasta sauce, and soup. Sure, you can buy these items pre-made, and I encourage you to find brands that are organic and use fresh, local ingredients. But making your own food creates an important relationship between it and you, and I think that's crucial when trying to understand what makes your body tick. Plus, you know exactly what's in there. For these reasons, I recommend investing in a good food processor.

Blender. In my opinion, a blender is a must-have—there are at least half a dozen smoothies listed in this book. I use a Vitamix, and personally, would never be able to go back to a regular blender. (Yup—I'm a blender snob.) If you want to be able to make fresh soup or sorbet in less than five minutes, get yourself a good quality, high-powered blender. They're more expensive, but in my opinion, totally worth it. (No, I'm not getting paid to endorse Vitamix. I just really, *really* love mine. Like, *a lot*.)

Juicer. This is essential if you want to make your own juice. There are many different makes and models out there, but I own a Breville Juice Fountain Compact. It was $149.00 from my neighborhood department store, and I use it so much it owes me nothing. As I've tweeted in the past, my juicer is well-traveled because I have a hard time skipping my morning juice. If you haven't started juicing already, you'll see what I'm raving about when you begin—the effects are almost immediate, and completely impressive.

Mixer. When it comes to baking, my mixer is my best friend. I love throwing ingredients into the bowl, flipping a switch, and walking away for a minute. I might not be getting the arm workout I used to, but it definitely makes baking more enjoyable. Who needs biceps when baking's a breeze?

Good knife set. I list this, because I've had knives that are crappy and knives that are amazing—and there is a colossal difference between the two. If you make your own food, then that means you spend a decent amount of time with a knife in your hand.

(Which might actually explain why my husband gets so nervous around me during meal times.) Why not cut down on that time, or at least make it more enjoyable? I recommend starting a great collection with a paring, Santoku, and chef's knife—those are the three you'll probably use the most.

Cast iron skillet. I recommend having two different sizes of these. Many people think that cast iron is difficult to cook with, because they're not non-stick. But guess what? If you care for them properly, they *are* non-stick. The secret is to layer the oil or fat you're using. After using, wash and dry immediately (but don't use soap), and then coat with coconut oil and store it like that. This will prevent your pan from rusting and keep it seasoned and greased up. When you go to cook with it (even eggs), add a second layer of fat such as grape seed oil or organic butter. When the pan gets hot, begin cooking. It will be totally non-stick, and a breeze to clean after. One giant bonus to cooking with cast iron is that you'll actually add extra iron to the food you prepare. Since most North Americans are at least a little bit anemic, this is a good way to inject more of that particular mineral into your diet.

Stainless steel, high-rimmed baking sheets. I use these to bake with, obviously, but also to press no-bake recipes into, too. (Like the Dark Chocolate Bars with Himalayan Sea Salt, page 178, or the Apricot Bars, page 186.) I own three in three different sizes, and use them all the time.

Spring-release ice-cream scoop. Ironically, not used for ice cream. I use a scoop for cookies, muffins, lentil "meat" balls, you name it. It makes everything faster and easier and less messy, which I love. I own three sizes, but honestly, I only really use the small and medium. Invest in those sizes, first.

Stainless steel whisk (two sizes). I also use these all the time—they are completely necessary for a ton of the recipes in this book (I mean, you could use a fork, but it doesn't work nearly as well), and very much underrated by most. Whisks are great for making your own salad dressings.

Microplane cheese grater. It's great to have one of these to use for hard cheese like fresh Parmesan, but also for citrus zesting, which is what I mostly use it for. Zesting orange, lemon, and lime peel is a snap with this contraption, and the microplane style lets you hold it flat over a recipe so that whether it's fruit or cheese, the pretty little curls fall just so for fab presentation.

Cleansing 101

"The road to health is paved with good intestines!"[4]
—Sherry A. Rogers, MD, Author

I'm aware that it might be a little odd to include a section on cleansing in a recipe book, but hear me out: preparing and consuming good quality foods for your body is really important, but so is giving your body a break from digesting those foods. Sometimes, for various reasons, we need a day or two to clean the pipes (so to speak), and this is where cleansing comes in.

Many people believe they understand what cleansing is, but honestly, I wasn't quite sure until I really researched it myself. I used to think that drinking water all day pretty much nailed it, but I was wrong. Here's why: cleansing isn't about starving your body for an extended period of time to drop five pounds before the weekend. (Which is what I used to think it was for, and it worked, but it wasn't very healthy.) It's about giving your digestive system a break while attempting to clean your colon out, for the purpose of increased nutrient absorption. There are many reasons why people feel the need to cleanse.

The question of why:
1. You're chronically exhausted. This kind of goes hand-in-hand with the second reason on this list. If you're tired all the time, chances are high that your digestive system is being sluggish or you're not absorbing the necessary nutrients you need for sustainable energy. If the gut is slow, you'll be slow, too. Cleansing can help this problem.
2. You're beyond constipated. *Soooo* many people fall into this category. If you're not moving your bowels at least once a day, then you're harboring waste that needs an exit strategy, pronto. Cleansing can help loosen debris and clear your gastrointestinal (GI) tract.
3. You're always getting sick. Since most of our immune system is in our gut, an inefficient digestive system equals compromised immunity. By cleaning out your intestinal

tract, you will give your immune system a much-needed boost.

4. You're exhibiting a variety of ailments that aren't being controlled by other means. Seemingly unrelated health issues, such as skin breakouts, depression, insomnia, and inflammation can all be traced back to GI health. Cleansing can help clear your system, and resolve many of these ailments without the need for medication.

5. You had too much fun in Mexico. Or Vegas. Or during the holidays. Or just in general. (Been there, done that—all of it.) A week or month or any extended period of over-indulgence can contribute to the need for cleaning out your digestive system, and giving it a wake-up call.

How does this work?

You may think that abstaining from solid foods for a day might be enough, but it's not. Cleaning house from the inside out involves removal of anything that contributes to a clogged tummy, and the malabsorption of necessary nutrients. If you just remove everything, you're not helping your body. You might be giving it a break, but your goal should be to remove the crap (literally) while simultaneously injecting the necessary micro-nutrients that are responsible for restoration. Keeping this in mind, here's what you should be mindful about consuming while you cleanse:

1. Water. It can come in the form of fresh-pressed juice or herbal tea, but you're going to need a decent amount of clear fluids.

2. Vitamins. A huge injection of various vitamins and antioxidants will be better absorbed through liquid than through solid foods. If you're going to be consuming a lot of liquid, why not make it the most nutritious liquid you can? This is where fresh-pressed fruit and vegetable juices come in. That is, juice you press yourself and drink immediately. Again, you'll need a juicer for this, folks. Bonus shots of wheatgrass are also great to incorporate.

3. Electrolytes. So . . . salt. But not table salt. You shouldn't even have this highly processed version in your home. Drinking filtered water with a pinch of sea salt will do the job, or better yet, drink organic miso broth. It's better because it's super high in electrolytes, and also digestive enzymes. You can also get electrolytes from pure, unsweetened coconut water.

4. Sugar. Again, I'm not suggesting you throw back tablespoons of sugar. The sugar you need will come from fresh-pressed juice, and you need it for the carbohydrates (energy) that it provides you with.

5. Variety. Don't just drink water and juice carrots. You need a large variation of fruits and vegetables on the day of your cleanse.

Tips for a successful cleanse:
1. Choose a day when you will be home, especially if you've never done this before. Your body may react in an unexpected way—it's kind of like Christmas for your bowel. (So exciting! Anything could happen! Lots of surprises!)
2. Plan ahead. Buy your groceries the day before, and make sure your juicer is clean and ready to go. About a week before your cleanse (even if you're only doing one day), begin weaning your body off alcohol, caffeine, processed foods, meat, dairy, sugar, and wheat. Your body will have an easier time adjusting to liquids for twenty-four hours if you prepare it for purity.
3. You will have better success if you drink a lot of water and tea throughout the day while you're cleansing. It will help keep your stomach full, and your skin detoxing.
4. Buy organic produce. The idea is to have as much nutrient absorption as possible by consuming only liquids, so why buy produce that is covered in pesticides? Try and stick to organic stuff only.
5. Have planned activities at home to keep you busy (like a giant puzzle or a fabulous book), but don't do anything strenuous that will make you extra hungry (like working out). Walking is good; just don't stray too far from home. (For obvious reasons—I have a story about this, but I'll spare you the details.)
6. Don't make food for other family members if you can avoid it. The temptation to chow down has proven too great for me many, many times.
7. Don't worry about protein. This is a low-protein day, but that's okay. You can fill up on protein-rich foods the next day.
8. If you feel shaky and cold on the day of your cleanse (which is totally normal, especially if you're doing this during the winter), try taking a bath with Epsom salts. The salt will help your body to detox further and the warm water will feel really good and calm your confused nerves. Remember, your body becomes addicted to things like caffeine and sugar just like it would any other drug. You're going to go through withdrawal, and it might be tough. But you can do it!

The plan:
7:00am: Eight ounces of warm water with half a lemon squeezed into it.
8:00am: Juice (in the following order): one chunk ginger, four carrots, and one peeled grapefruit.

10:00am:	Juice (in the following order): two green apples, four fennel fronds, six romaine lettuce leaves, handful of parsley, and one large cucumber.
12:00pm:	Eight ounces of organic miso broth.
2:00pm:	Juice (in the following order): one chunk ginger, one small beet, two large carrots, two red apples, handful of basil, and one large cucumber.
4:00pm:	Eight ounces of unsweetened coconut water.
6:00pm:	Blend (in the following order): one cup water, one banana, four kale leaves, one cup spinach, one cup frozen pineapple, and a half cup of rolled oats.

In addition to everything above, try to drink extra water or herbal tea throughout the day if you get hungry or thirsty. The last "meal" is more solid, because it will help you to sleep better on a fuller stomach, and create a bit of bulk for a good bowel movement in the morning.

The shopping list:
Fruit
- One lemon
- Six carrots
- One grapefruit
- Two green apples
- Two red apples
- One banana
- Two thumbs ginger
- Two cups frozen pineapple

Veggies
- Fennel (with at least four fronds)
- One small bunch romaine

- One small bunch kale
- One small bunch spinach
- One small bunch fresh parsley
- One small bunch fresh basil
- Two cucumbers
- One beet

*Repeat this for up to two days if you want, but I don't recommend detoxing for longer than that, unless you have prior experience with cleanses.

Other

- One cup rolled oats
- Eight ounces miso broth (buy in packets in health food aisle)
- Herbal tea
- Eight ounces unsweetened coconut water
- Epsom salts (for a bath)

"Every human being is the author of his own health or disease."[5]
—Buddha

JUICE

The term "juicing" refers to making your own fresh-pressed juice. I'm not talking about purchasing frozen, concentrated juice mix and adding water. I'm talking about taking fresh, organic fruits and vegetables, running them through a juicer, then immediately drinking the fresh, frothy concoction that you've just made. Sound like a lot of work? It's not!

When you consume fresh juice, you are absorbing raw, living enzymes that are necessary for good health. Because it's in liquid form, it's already super easy to digest, and all of those living nutrients can make their way easily and immediately into your gut. It's also a great way to get tons of antioxidants into your body in a short period of time. You would never consume a beet, four carrots, two apples, a few celery stalks, a couple of lettuce leaves, and a chunk of ginger for a meal, would you? Probably not. But you can juice all of that into about twenty ounces of liquid and drink it up in under two minutes.

Those who aren't giant fans of juicing usually feel this way because it involves the removal of fiber. Essentially, juicing your breakfast means that the beautiful fruits and veggies are no longer consumed as whole foods. However, fresh juice gives you great hydration, an immediate influx of much-needed nutrients, and is usually processed by your body effectively, even if you have a digestive disorder. For those who have trouble getting enough vitamins, juicing is a great way to aid your body in nutrient absorption. Many people suffering from severe GI problems have a hard time digesting fiber. Because juicing removes the fiber, it's easier on the gut to process.

When you juice, try to use organic ingredients. Juicing is a great way to absorb mass amounts of nutrients, so you may as well maximize the nutritional benefits and minimize the pesticide absorption. Also, always juice the ingredients in order of least juicy to most. For example, roots go first (like ginger and beets), then leaves second (like romaine, kale, and spinach), then fruit next, and then cucumbers last. This way, the nutrients from the first foods get flushed all the way out by the last ones. Juice the following recipes in the order that the ingredients are given.

Each recipe makes 12–16 ounces of gorgeously glorious juice.

Anti-Inflammatory Juice (v) (V) (GF)

Ingredients

1 thumb of ginger

6 romaine lettuce leaves

2 green apples

4 fennel stalks with fronds

1 cucumber

Classic Green Juice (v) (V) (GF)

Ingredients

Handful of fresh mint leaves

Handful of spinach

4 kale leaves

2 green apples

1 cucumber

Smooth Juice (v) (V) (GF)

Ingredients

2 green apples

1 cup strawberries

1 orange

2 cups watermelon

Sweet Pink Juice (v) (V) (GF)

Ingredients

1 small beet

2 carrots

4 romaine lettuce leaves

2 red apples

1 cucumber

Sweet Pink Juice

Anti-Inflammatory Juice

Pumped Up Juice (v) (V) (GF)

Ingredients

1 small thumb of ginger

4 kale leaves

4 pineapple spears

1 cucumber

8 ml. strong, cold green tea

*Juice first four ingredients, then add green
   tea to juice at the end. Stir and enjoy!

Breakfast Juice (v) (V) (GF)

Ingredients

1 thumb of ginger

1 large pink grapefruit

4 large carrots

Green Goddess Juice (v) (V) (GF)

Ingredients

3 carrots

3 kale leaves

Handful of parsley

2 red apples

2 celery stalks

1 cucumber

½ lemon (squeezed over top)

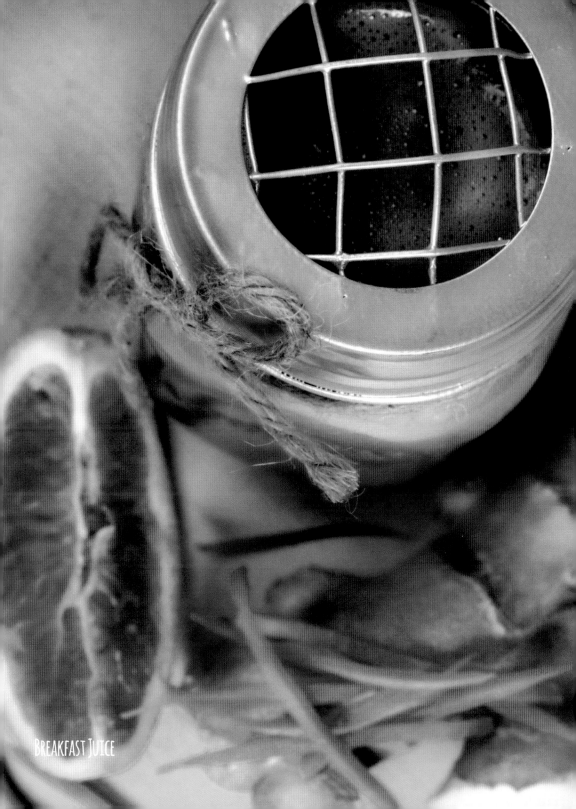

Breakfast Juice

"A smoothie a day keeps Big Pharma away."[6]
—Gary Hopkins, author

Smoothies

All Hail King Kale Smoothie (p. 52)

For those who are prone to constipation and desperately need the fiber, blending can be a life-saver. Like juicing, blending is a fabulous way to give your body large amounts of raw, fresh nutrients in a smaller-sized snack. I'll often blend water, a banana, a cucumber, kale, and some frozen pineapple together for a delicious snack that is, obviously, very nutrient-dense. Smoothies are more filling than juices and the main difference between the two is that when you blend, you get the whole food including the fiber. Something that I have recently begun to do is save the fiber from my juicer and add it to the blender when I'm making a smoothie. That way, no fiber gets wasted and my smoothies are extra-nutritious!

America is constipated. To help flush out the colon and aid in building a healthy digestive system, fiber is beyond necessary. Blending whole foods that are high in fiber every day can dramatically help this situation.

And don't be afraid to think outside the box when it comes to ingredients. Although it's easier for people who own high-powered blenders to end up with a smoother, more consistent result, don't feel like you can't experiment if you have a regular blender. I've thrown things in my smoothies that other people think are super weird, like pitted dates, pomegranate seeds (this one is *only* for a high-powered blender), and raw oats. They *do* blend, and they add fiber (dates), antioxidants (pomegranate seeds), and protein (raw oats) to my smoothies. And believe me, those drinks are *delish.*

Why pay up to ten dollars for a good smoothie at a smoothie stand when you can make your own, exactly the way you like it?! Smoothies are a part of my daily routine. They're the ultimate "fast food," and are stellar for a post-workout snack. I urge you to try as many as you can—you never know when you might stumble across something deliciously magical.

Blend the following smoothies in the order in which the ingredients are listed. They're all (albeit huge) single-servings, and they'll all rock your world.

Strawberry-Banana Smoothie

Each recipe makes 16–24 ounces of seriously succulent smoothie.

Strawberry-Banana Smoothie (v) (V) (GF)

This is my family's favorite. Who can improve on strawberries and bananas?

Ingredients

1 cup water

1 banana

10 frozen strawberries

5 raw walnut halves

Method

Combine all ingredients except walnuts in blender. Blend for thirty seconds. Pour into a tall glass, and sprinkle with walnuts. (You might want to serve with a spoon.) Substitute the water for unsweetened soy milk if you would like a more calorie-dense smoothie for meal replacement purposes.

Berry-Rhubarb Smoothie (v) (V) (GF)

Despite the fact that rhubarb is tart, this smoothie is anything but. It's a great way to take advantage of fresh rhubarb once it makes its appearance at your local farmer's market or grocery store—it's definitely an early spring, seasonal goodie.

Ingredients

1½ cups unsweetened almond milk

1 cup chopped, fresh rhubarb

1 cup frozen mixed berries

1 tsp. cinnamon

Method

Place all ingredients in blender and blend until smooth. Enjoy!

All Hail King Kale Smoothie (v) (V) (GF)

This smoothie will help you get your kale on, without you even tasting it. Even my picky kiddies enjoy this one!

Ingredients

1 cup water

3 kale leaves

1 banana

1 cup frozen pineapple

Method

Place all ingredients into blender, and blend until smooth. Drink immediately.

Rockin' Raspberry Smoothie (v) (V) (GF)

Again, you would never dream this smoothie contains spinach. It's a fabulous way to increase your iron, while tricking your brain into thinking you're all about the fruit.

Ingredients

1 cup water

1 banana

Handful of fresh spinach

½ cup frozen raspberries

½ cup frozen mango chunks

Method

Place all ingredients into blender and blend until smooth. Drink immediately.

Tropicana Smoothie (v) (V) (GF)

This smoothie is like a mini vacation in a cup.

Ingredients

1 cup unsweetened coconut water

1 banana

2 pineapple spears

½ cup frozen mango chunks

Method

Combine all ingredients in blender, blend until smooth, and drink immediately.

Protein Blast Smoothie (v) (V) (GF)

Want to add a little more protein to your snack? This smoothie is for you.

Ingredients

1 cup unsweetened, organic soy milk

¼ cup gluten-free rolled oats

1 scoop natural hemp protein powder

1 tsp. white chia seeds

1 tsp. ground flaxseed

1 large frozen banana

1 cup frozen peaches

Method

Combine all ingredients in blender and blend until smooth. Drink immediately.

Protein Blast Smoothie

Chunky Monkey Smoothie (V) (V) (GF)

This one's for those with a little bit of a sweet tooth—it's basically dessert in a cup. (Shhh . . .) To make it less sweet, simply eliminate the dates.

Ingredients

1 cup unsweetened almond milk

1 large frozen banana (peeled)

1 tbsp. nut butter (peanut or almond)

½ cup gluten-free rolled oats

4 pitted dates

½ tbsp. unsweetened cocoa powder

½ cup ice

Method

Combine all ingredients in blender and blend until smooth. Drink immediately.

Superhero Smoothie (V) (V) (GF)

This smoothie is absolutely teeming with vitamins. It makes a fab lunch replacement!

Ingredients

1 cup water

1 tbsp. agave syrup

2 cups fresh spinach

¾ cup frozen blueberries

1 tbsp. chia seeds

Method

Combine all ingredients into blender in the order listed above. Blend for one minute. Drink up!

CHUNKY MONKEY SMOOTHIE

"Today, much of the challenge of eating well comes
down to choosing real food."[7]
—Michael Pollan, *Food Rules*

Sauces & Dressings

The recipes in this section are ones that I just can't live without, because they accompany so many of my staple meals! Store-bought sauces and dressings are typically *the worst*, because they are absolutely loaded with extra oil, salt, and sugar, not to mention all of those ingredients that are completely unpronounceable. The amount of additives and preservatives in most commercial preparations is astounding, and totally unnecessary. So make your own, instead! I use these constantly, and saucy things are yummy, so here you go.

BASIC DRESSING Makes 1½ cups (v) (V) (GF)

Wanna know a secret? I use this dressing to drizzle on steamed veggies, too.

INGREDIENTS	METHOD
1 cup extra virgin olive oil	Combine all ingredients in a food processor and blend on high for 10 seconds. It will keep on the counter, out of the sun, for approximately one week. Stir well before using each time.
½ cup white wine vinegar	
Handful of flat Italian parsley	
2 garlic cloves	
1 shallot	

BALSAMIC VINAIGRETTE Makes 1 cup (v) (V) (GF)

This dressing has a little kick. If you suffer from GERD, omit the cayenne.

INGREDIENTS	METHOD
¼ cup balsamic vinegar ½ cup extra virgin olive oil 1 tbsp. Dijon mustard 1 tsp. cayenne pepper 1 tbsp. maple syrup	Combine all ingredients and mix well. It will keep on the counter, out of the sun, for approximately two weeks. Stir well before using each time.

DILL DRESSING Makes 1 cup (v) (GF)

To make vegan, substitute the Greek yogurt for soy yogurt.

INGREDIENTS	METHOD
¼ cup organic, plain Greek yogurt	Blend first five ingredients in food processor until smooth. Slowly add oil with the food processor running, continuing to blend for ten seconds after all oil is added. Add dill and pulse until mixed. Place in airtight container and store in fridge for up to one week. Re-whisk before each use.
2 garlic cloves	
2 tbsp. Dijon mustard	
2 tbsp. rice vinegar	
1 tbsp. lime juice	
¼ cup olive oil	
¼ cup fresh dill, chopped	

Spicy Miso Sesame Dressing Makes ½ cup (v) (V) (GF)

This dressing packs some heat. Remember, it's a good burn.

Ingredients	Method
2 tbsp. miso paste	Combine all ingredients except sesame seeds in food processor and blend until smooth. Stir in sesame seeds. Cover and refrigerate for up to a week. Whisk before each use.
2 tbsp. rice vinegar	
1 tbsp. sesame oil	
1 tbsp. honey	
1 tsp. wasabi paste	
1½ tsp. lime juice	
1 tsp. fresh ginger, minced	
1 tsp. sesame seeds	

ORIENTAL DRESSING Makes about ⅔ cup (v) (V) (GF)

The flavor of the almond butter is what gives this dressing its *je ne sais quoi.*

INGREDIENTS	METHOD
⅓ cup rice vinegar 1 tbsp. almond butter 1 tbsp. Dijon mustard 1 tsp. lemon juice 1 tsp. sesame seeds ½ tsp. minced ginger ½ tsp. minced garlic ¼ tsp. sea salt ¼ cup extra virgin olive oil	Place all ingredients except oil in blender and blend until smooth. Slowly add in extra virgin olive oil until desired consistency is reached. Cover and refrigerate. Will keep for about a week.

BOSS SAUCE Makes 1 cup (v) (V) (GF)

I use it like a boss—I put it on *everything*. It's a great topping for steamed veggies, and makes a fantastic sandwich spread. (A great alternative to hummus, basically.)

Ingredients	Method
¾ cup raw walnuts	Place all ingredients except for sesame seeds in food processor and blend until smooth. Depending on the desired consistency, you may want to add a little more or less water. Once you've added this sauce to your favorite food, sprinkle the sesame seeds on top to make it pretty. Store in an airtight container in the refrigerator for 2–3 days.
¼ cup tahini	
2 tbsp. tamari	
2 tbsp. water	
1 tbsp. minced garlic	
1 tbsp. sesame seeds	

PERFECT PESTO Makes 1 cup (v) (V) (GF)

Perfect Pesto is so versatile. You can use it for spreads, dips, pasta and/or pizza sauce, and even salad dressing. Your life will be less boring with this Perfect Pesto recipe in it—*I promise.*

INGREDIENTS	METHOD
2 cups fresh basil leaves 1 cup fresh spinach 6 garlic cloves, minced ⅓ cup pine nuts ½ cup avocado oil ½ tsp. sea salt	Combine basil, spinach, garlic, and pine nuts in food processor. Blend until slightly chunky. Slowly add oil to mixture, blending on low until fully immersed. Remove from processor, and mix by hand a few times. Add sea salt to taste, and a little water to achieve a thinner consistency, if desired. Store in an airtight container in the refrigerator for up to a week.

TZATZIKI Makes about 2½ cups (v) (V) (GF)

INGREDIENTS	METHOD
1½ cups medium-firm tofu 2 tbsp. lemon juice 1 tbsp. white wine vinegar 3 garlic cloves, minced 2 tbsp. olive oil 1 cup grated cucumber 1 tbsp. fresh mint, minced Salt and pepper to taste (optional)	Add tofu, lemon juice, vinegar, garlic, and oil to food processor. Blend until smooth. Place grated cucumber in cheesecloth or paper towel and wring out as much moisture as possible. Add cucumber and mint to food processor and pulse a few times until thoroughly incorporated. Add salt and/or pepper to taste, if desired. Transfer to bowl and refrigerate for two hours to let it thicken up before serving. If you have leftovers, store in an airtight container in the refrigerator for up to a week.

TAHINI DIPPING SAUCE Serves 4 (v) (V) (GF)

Use this sauce for a delicious spread in sandwiches, burgers, and wraps.

INGREDIENTS	METHOD
2 garlic cloves	Blend garlic, herbs, salt, and lemon juice in food processor. Add water and tahini and process until smooth. Store in an airtight container in the refrigerator for up to a week.
½ cup basil *or* cilantro	
½ tsp. sea salt	
2 tbsp. lemon juice	
½ cup water	
½ cup tahini paste	

———————————————————————

I love breakfast, and so should you. No one should ever skip it—it exists for a reason. If your desire is to become healthier and have more energy and create better eating habits for yourself, you can start by making sure you don't skip breakfast, which literally means "breaking the fast." It doesn't have to be a big meal; even a juice or a smoothie will do the trick.

Wake & Break

BLONDE MUESLI serves 1 (v) (V) (GF)

This pretty breakfast is magic for your taste buds. It's easy to make, super nutritious, and kicks store-bought cereal's *butt*. (Conventional cereal being extremely high in sugar and very low in actual nutrients.) You can even make it the night before, minus the pear and almond milk, and just add those two ingredients right before eating. Or, you can make it all and just eat it cold the next day, which I've done a billion times. (Okay, probably more like a dozen.)

Ingredients	Method
½ cup gluten-free rolled oats	Layer ingredients in the listed order in a bowl. Eat immediately!
2 tbsp. ground flaxseeds	
¼ cup shredded coconut	
1 tbsp. white chia seeds	
½ cup unsweetened almond milk	
½ pear, sliced thinly	
Cinnamon to taste	

BANANA-WALNUT PANCAKES Makes 4 large (v) (V) (GF)

These pancakes taste like banana bread. They are heavy and delicious and as healthy as pancakes come. Swap the quinoa flour for another kind if you want (oat flour is awesome), but I use quinoa to pump up the protein and create a nutty-tasting result. Whichever flour you choose, they'll be delicious. Also, you can make a couple of batches ahead of time, freeze them individually, and then pop them in the toaster whenever you want to eat up!

INGREDIENTS	METHOD
1¼ cups unsweetened almond milk	Whisk together non-dairy milk, mashed banana, and vanilla extract. Set aside. In a separate bowl, mix together the flour, oats, baking powder, baking soda, and cinnamon. Incorporate the dry ingredients into the wet, and mix until just combined.
1 large banana, mashed	
1 tsp. vanilla extract	
1 cup quinoa flour	
⅓ cup gluten-free rolled oats	Melt coconut oil in a non-stick pan (I use ceramic) over medium heat. Add about a half-cup of the batter into the pan. Flip once bubbles have formed and popped (approximately 2–3 minutes per side). Top with fresh banana, walnuts, and syrup. Yum!
1 tsp. aluminum-free baking powder	
1 tsp. baking soda	
½ tsp. cinnamon	
1 tbsp. coconut oil	
½ cup banana slices	
¼ cup chopped walnuts	
2 tbsp. maple syrup	

#LifeIsPeachy Pudding serves 4 (v) (V) (GF)

A twist on conventional oatmeal! I actually make this for myself sans syrup, but
my kids like it better with. (Shocker.) It produces a high-energy breakfast that is
great in the summer when peaches are in season. If making in the winter, you
can swap the peaches for dried apricots.

Ingredients	Method
2 cups gluten-free rolled oats	Combine oats, ⅔ cup of the coconut, coconut milk, and
1 cup unsweetened shredded	nutmeg in pot. Bring to a slight boil, then reduce to a
coconut	simmer, cover, and cook for about 10 minutes. Remove from
3 cups unsweetened	heat, divide into four bowls, and top with peach slices and
coconut milk	remaining coconut. Drizzle with half a tablespoon of maple
¼ tsp. nutmeg	syrup. Enjoy!
1 peach, sliced	
2 tbsp. maple syrup	

Breakfast Quinoa with Honey & Bananas

Serves 2 (v) (V) (GF)

This is another great alternative to a hot breakfast cereal. Breakfast should not be boring! The walnuts add some healthy fat, and quinoa is a complete protein, which creates a perfect meal for plant-based eaters. Eat up!

Ingredients	Method
1 cup quinoa 2 cups unsweetened almond milk 1 banana, sliced ¼ cup chopped walnuts 1 tbsp. cinnamon	Combine quinoa and almond milk. Bring to a simmer on the stove, then turn heat down to low. Cook until all milk is absorbed and quinoa is fairly translucent. Remove from heat and divide into bowls. Top with banana slices, walnuts, and cinnamon. Enjoy!

DENVER "EGGS" Serves 3 (v) (V) (GF)

That's right—the eggs are actually soy-based! And they're *so good*. It takes no time at all to make, and will fool even the fussiest of eaters. You would never know that these are not actual scrambled eggs. (My husband didn't!) Man, I love the versatility of tofu.

INGREDIENTS	METHOD
1 cup extra-firm tofu	Crumble tofu, press with paper towel to release excess liquid, and set aside. Mince garlic, dice onion and pepper, slice mushrooms, and tear spinach. Heat frying pan over medium heat and add oil. Once hot, add garlic and onion to pan and let soften (about 2–3 minutes). Add tofu and remaining vegetables to pan and mix. Add tamari and chili powder.
1 tbsp. avocado oil	
2 cloves garlic	
½ red onion	
1 medium red bell pepper	
5 mushrooms	
½ cup fresh spinach	Sauté over medium heat, using a spatula to move mixture around in the pan until it resembles scrambled eggs and is hot (about 5 minutes). Remove from heat and stir in yeast. Serve hot with sprouted grain toast or fruit.
1 tbsp. tamari	
1 tsp. chili powder	
1 tsp. nutritional yeast	

BREAKFAST RANCHEROS Serves 3 (v) (V)

Love a great breakfast wrap? Me too! I love eating with my hands, so this one's a goodie. You can choose to use either organic corn or whole grain tortillas (or brown rice tortillas if you're gluten-free), but either way, it's much better if you warm them first (especially if you're using corn). Come hungry, and make sure you have a napkin (or five) handy.

INGREDIENTS	METHOD
1 batch Denver "Eggs" (recipe on page 78) ¾ cup Fresh Salsa (page 94) ½ cup chopped cilantro 3 large organic corn, whole grain, or brown rice tortillas	Warm tortillas. Fill with "eggs", salsa, and cilantro. Roll up wrap and eat immediately! For extra calories and overall yumminess, serve each with ¼ cup of Karley's Famous Guacamole (page 99) on the side.

"OM" OATMEAL **Serves 2 (v) (V) (GF)**

This breakfast will keep your tummy full for hours, and is high in both protein and overall yumminess.

INGREDIENTS	METHOD
1 cup gluten-free rolled oats 2 tbsp. hemp hearts ¼ cup dried dates 1 tsp. ground flaxseed 1½ cups water Pumpkin and sunflower seeds to garnish	Throw the first four ingredients into a small stainless steel pot and combine. Add water to just cover the oat mixture (about 1½ cups). Cook on low-medium heat until water is absorbed; about 5 minutes. (Stir a few times throughout.) Remove from stove and scoop into two bowls. Garnish with pumpkin and sunflower seeds.

HOMEMADE GRANOLA   Makes about 2 cups (v) (V) (GF)

This is great to serve on top of soy yogurt, with a splash of almond milk, or to throw on top of fruit salad. Even on its own, this granola is delicious, and a far cry from the processed granola you find in stores. I usually keep some in a sealed container in my car so that I can snack when I'm on the road. (And I'm a literal Kid Cab, so I'm in my vehicle *a lot*.)

INGREDIENTS	METHOD
2 tbsp. coconut oil	Lay out about one foot of parchment paper. Slowly melt coconut oil in large pot over low heat. Add honey, vanilla, and cinnamon. Whisk until well blended together, then remove pot from burner.
1½ tbsp. honey	
½ tsp. vanilla	
1 tsp. cinnamon	
1 cup gluten-free rolled oats	In a bowl, mix oats, pecans, and pumpkin seeds, then add to the honey mixture. Return pot to burner, and mix until coated. Turn heat up to medium-high. Stir mixture for about 5 minutes, or until slightly toasted.
⅓ cup raw pecan pieces or halves	
⅓ cup raw, salted pumpkin seeds	Turn off heat, and stir in raisins (if you're not a raisin lover, then just omit them). Spread mixture out on parchment paper to cool. Once cooled completely, store in an airtight container. Granola should keep on the counter for at least a week.
¼ cup raisins (optional)	

Fresh Fruit Salad with Mint Serves 1 (v) (GF)

This is a very pretty fruit salad. It goes nicely with a fruit smoothie, resulting in a huge helping of micronutrients. To make a heartier version, you can top the Greek yogurt with a handful of Homemade Granola (page 83). To make this recipe completely vegan, substitute the Greek yogurt for soy yogurt.

Ingredients	Method
6 strawberries	Slice the fresh fruit and chop the mint. Layer fruit, yogurt, and mint in dish or jar in the order given. Enjoy!
1 peach	
1 banana	
¼ cup chopped dates	
¼ cup plain Greek yogurt	
6 mint leaves	

"I really used to eat a lot of crap, and now I don't, and I feel great, and I absolutely love healthy food."[9]
—Ellen Page, actor

Here's the deal: I'm a snacker—I graze. I'm totally incapable of only eating three times a day and have found that healthy snacks provide much-needed energy just when I need it most. You don't have to feel guilty about snacking if you're eating the right foods, and I can prove it with the following recipes.

The first two you'll see here were created by my amazing sister-in-law, who has a much better imagination when it comes to assembling these creations than I do. She's an incredible chef and has no fear when it comes to experimenting with new food. Natalie Browne—thank you so much for these contributions. (I know readers will want to thank you, too.)

NIBBLES

PISTACHIO STUFFED FIGS Makes 24 (v) (V) (GF)

The first time my sister-in-law made these, I ate about a dozen. No joke; they're that good. Thank goodness they're perfectly pure, because otherwise, this recipe would be a big problem. (You know—for my hips.) Also, if you're a lazy cook (like I am), you don't even have to bake these. I've eaten them both ways, and both ways are delicious. *I can almost feel my sister-in-law rolling her eyes . . .*

INGREDIENTS	METHOD
¾ cup shelled pistachios 24 dried figs 2 tsp. dried cardamom 1 tsp. cumin 1 orange, zest only	Preheat oven to 350 degrees Fahrenheit. Over low heat, toast pistachios until golden. Remove from heat and allow to cool slightly until you're able to handle them. While the pistachios are toasting, slice the figs three quarters of the way through, and set aside. Finely chop the pistachios and place in a small mixing bowl. Mix in the cardamom, cumin, and orange zest. Spoon the pistachio mixture into the figs, patting it down as you go. Place the figs on a baking sheet and bake for 8–10 minutes until warm and slightly sticky. Serve immediately. *Recipe contributed by Natalie Browne of *Kitchen, Uncorked.*

Roasted Vegetable Bruschetta Makes 12-16 (v)

We've all had the traditional tomato-based bruschetta, and yes, it's amazing. You want to know what's even better? *This variation*. A lovely twist on an old favorite—and that's large praise coming from me, because I could totally live off traditional bruschetta. (But it looks like I won't have to.) To make this vegan, omit the goat cheese.

Ingredients

1 large zucchini

1 Japanese eggplant

3 tbsp. extra virgin olive oil

12 cherry tomatoes

½ head of garlic

1 lemon, juice only

1 tbsp. dried basil

1 tbsp. dried oregano

Salt and pepper to taste

1 whole grain baguette, sliced
  into rounds

2 tbsp. goat cheese (optional)

Method

Preheat the oven to 375 degrees Fahrenheit. Slice zucchini and eggplant into half-inch circles and toss gently with 2 tbsp. of the olive oil. Place single-layer on a baking sheet and add tomatoes and garlic. Drizzle vegetables with remaining olive oil. Bake for 25–30 minutes until tender, and then allow to sit for 10 minutes.

Once the veggies are cool(ish), dice the cooked zucchini and eggplant and place into a mixing bowl. Remove the skin from the tomatoes and garlic. Roughly chop and add to the same mixing bowl. Add the lemon juice, basil, oregano, salt, and pepper. Gently stir.

Place baguette rounds on a baking sheet in a single layer. Spread the mixture onto baguette slices and bake for about 10 minutes until heated through. Once done, remove from oven, top each slice with goat cheese (or don't), and enjoy!

*Recipe contributed by Natalie Browne of *Kitchen, Uncorked.*

Layered Dip, Two Ways:

MEXICAN SEVEN-LAYER DIP Makes about 4 cups (v) (GF)

Everyone loves a good dip. What's better to snack on than something you can scoop onto a tortilla chip or carrot stick?! Because I eat mainly plant-based, I'm crazy about beans, and they provide loads of protein and fiber, which are two things I try and track my intake of. Make sure that when and if you buy a can of refried beans, you check the ingredients to make sure that beans are the only thing in there—no added oils, salt, or anything else. To be extra-awesome, try and buy your beans BPA-free. Eden has great refried beans that come in a can that isn't lined with this chemical. Also, if you'd like to make this recipe entirely vegan, substitute the cheese for Daiya.

INGREDIENTS

1 cup Fresh Salsa (page 94)

1 cup refried beans

1 cup Karley's Famous
 Guacamole (page 99)

1 yellow bell pepper

½ cup sliced black olives

2 green onions

½ cup shredded Monterey Jack
 cheese

Raw veggies for dipping *or*
 gluten-free tortilla chips for
 scooping

METHOD

Combine salsa and refried beans. (This is so the beans aren't as dense, and the chips don't break.) Spread mixture in the bottom of an 8x8 square baking dish. Layer remaining ingredients in the order given. Serve with raw veggies or organic corn tortilla chips, and pretend you're in Mexico.

Greek Six-Layer Dip   **Makes approximately 4 cups (v) (V) (GF)**

A Greek version of the popular Mexican Seven-Layer Dip (page 92). Need I say more?

Ingredients	Method
1 cup vegan Tzatziki (see recipe on page 68) ½ cucumber 1 small red onion 1 orange bell pepper 2 Roma tomatoes ½ cup Kalamata olives Raw veggies for dipping	Dice the cucumber, onion, pepper, and tomatoes, and slice the olives. Layer ingredients in the order given in an 8x8 square baking dish (or any shallow dish this size). Serve cold with raw veggies.

Fresh Salsa Makes 2 cups (v) (V) (GF)

This stuff is to die for, and I use it on everything, all summer long. I also use it as a main "ingredient" in tons of the recipes in this book. Keep reading—you'll see.

Ingredients	Method
1 small red onion	Combine onion, bell pepper, and jalapeño in food processor. Pulse until roughly chopped. Add tomatoes and cilantro. Pulse until tomatoes are diced to your size preference. Add black beans, corn, juice from lime, and salt. Stir by hand. Serve with organic tortilla chips, and store in an airtight container in the refrigerator for up to a week.
1 yellow bell pepper	
1 small jalapeño pepper	
12 grape tomatoes	
½ cup of cilantro	
1 cup black beans	
½ cup organic corn	
1 lime	
½ tsp. sea salt	

KALE CHIPS Serves 2 (v) (V) (GF)

This is my absolute favorite way to eat kale. Because it feels naughty. Because I turned it into a chip.

INGREDIENTS	METHOD
1 bunch fresh kale 2 tbsp. olive oil ¼ tsp. nutritional yeast Sea salt to taste	Preheat oven to 350 degrees Fahrenheit. Wash and dry kale; rip into pieces. Place kale in large bowl, add olive oil, and mix by hand, coating kale well. Spread the kale out on a cookie sheet in a single layer. Grind sea salt lightly over top. Bake for approximately 8 minutes, until edges of kale are crisp-looking. Remove from heat and place on cooling rack. Evenly sprinkle nutritional yeast over the kale, and eat within a couple of hours. (But sooner is better.)

EGGPLANT PIZZA Serves 6 (v) (GF)

Eggplant makes a great alternative to a grain crust, and it's all veggie, baby.
Also, you can totally substitute the eggplant for zucchini if you want. Just
slice the zucchini down the middle to make two long halves. Scoop out the
middle, and fill with rest of ingredients. To make totally vegan, substitute
the goat cheese for Daiya, or simply leave out.

INGREDIENTS

1 small eggplant

2 tsp. sea salt

2 tbsp. olive oil

¼ cup tomato sauce

½ red onion

1 cup (assorted colors) grape
   tomatoes

Handful fresh basil

2 tbsp. goat cheese

METHOD

Preheat oven to 350 degrees Fahrenheit. Slice eggplant into
⅓ -inch rounds. (Should yield about 12–14 slices.) Sprinkle
a pinch of salt on both sides, and place on a clean dishtowel.
Let sit for 10 minutes to sweat out the moisture, then use
another clean dishtowel to press down on the rounds and
release any wetness that remains.

Arrange rounds on a large baking pan in a single layer, and
brush oil on top. Bake for about 7 minutes, then remove
from oven, flip rounds over, and brush other side with oil.
Bake another 5 minutes, and remove from oven again.

Slice the tomatoes and onion and chop the basil. Spread
thin layer of tomato sauce over rounds and top with onion,
tomatoes, basil, and goat cheese. Bake for approximately
7–10 more minutes. Remove from oven (last time,
I promise!), and enjoy as an appetizer or side dish
immediately.

KARLEY'S FAMOUS GUACAMOLE **Makes about 3 cups (v) (V) (GF)**

This guacamole was first introduced to me by my friend, Karley. While completely preventing me from enjoying any other guacamole *ever*, she also provided me with a great recipe for this book. So I guess I should say thank you. Thanks, Karley!

INGREDIENTS	METHOD
4 avocados	Peel and quarter avocados, chop into chunks, and place in bowl. Dice tomatoes and mince garlic and onion. Place in bowl. Chop cilantro and add to bowl along with lime juice and sea salt. Mix by hand, so that the guacamole is still fairly chunky. Serve with organic corn tortilla chips or fresh veggies. This will keep in the refrigerator in an airtight container for up to two days.
2 Roma tomatoes	
2 garlic cloves	
1 white onion	
1 cup chopped cilantro	
Juice of 1 lime	
Pinch of sea salt	
	*Recipe contributed by Karley Seabrook.

Spicy Roasted Nuts & Seeds Makes 2 cups (v) (V) (GF)

Freshen up your salads, oatmeal, and even casseroles with these spicy, roasted bits of heaven. If you're not a huge spice fan, then skip the cayenne. If you're brave and bold, double it.

Ingredients	Method
½ cup raw pecans	Lay one foot of parchment paper along counter. Heat frying pan on medium. Once hot, add nuts and seeds. Let roast while moving around for about 3–4 minutes, or until golden brown. Turn heat off, and add syrup, cinnamon, and cayenne to coat, tossing quickly.
½ cup raw pumpkin seeds	
½ cup raw sunflower seeds	
½ cup raw almonds	
¼ cup maple or agave syrup	
2 tbsp. cinnamon	Transfer to parchment paper in single layer. Let cool completely, then store in a glass jar until eaten. For me, they rarely last longer than a week. (Okay, a day.)
1 tsp. cayenne pepper	

HOLY HUMMUS (BECAUSE IT'S FROM THE HEAVENS)

Makes about 2 cups (v) (V) (GF)

I use this for everything from a dip for raw veggies and tortilla chips to a spread for sandwiches. So. Darn. Good.

INGREDIENTS	METHOD
1 16-oz. can of chickpeas	Place all ingredients except for paprika and sesame seeds in food processor. Pulse on low until chunky. If you need to add water, add by the tablespoon until desired consistency is reached, but the goal is to leave it a little gloopy. (Yes, that's a word.)
¼ cup tahini	
2 cloves garlic, minced	
Juice of 1 lemon	
2 tbsp. extra virgin olive oil	
1 tsp. sea salt	Scoop out of processor, place in dish, and sprinkle with sesame seeds and paprika. Store in an airtight container in the fridge for 4–5 days.
1 tsp. ground cumin	
Water to desired consistency (about 2 tbsp.)	
½ tsp. paprika	
1 tbsp. sesame seeds	

SPROUTED ENDIVE BOATS Makes approximately 16 (v) (V) (GF)

These cute little two-biters are super nutritious and look cool plated. They have tons of flavor, with the benefit of being wholesome and vegan. (My kinda tapa.) Note: Sometimes it's hard to find endive spears, so ask around.

INGREDIENTS	METHOD
1 carrot 2 endive spears 1 cup bean sprouts 2 tbsp. gluten-free tamari	Julienne the carrot and set aside. Peel layers off endive spears and arrange on platter so the cavities are face-up, resembling boats. Set aside. Place ¼ cup of water in skillet and heat to medium. Once simmering, add bean sprouts and sauté for 2 minutes to soften, slightly. Remove from heat and drain any remaining water. Add tamari to bean sprouts, toss to coat, and scoop into endive cavities. Garnish with 2–3 strips of carrot and serve.

NORI ROLL Serves 4 (v) (V) (GF)

This super simple, low-calorie snack is both easy to put together and fun to make. It's a great appetizer at parties, and equally as awesome as a quick lunch. Basically, it's the ultimate finger food.

Ingredients	Method
1 carrot	Julienne the carrot and cucumber, and thinly slice the avocado. Wet one sheet of nori, and place on smooth surface. Place ¼ cup brown rice on top, then layer ¼ of the veggies. Carefully roll the nori up, wrap-style. Repeat with the rest of the ingredients. Dip rolls in tamari for each bite for added flavor.
1 cucumber	
1 avocado	
4 sheets nori	
1 cup cooked brown rice	
½ cup gluten-free tamari	

"True healthcare reform starts in
your kitchen, not in Washington."[10]
—Anonymous

What's a great meal without sides? More than any other type of food, vegetarian fare prides itself on insanely flavorful side dishes—and these are ones you will want to make over and over again.

Sides

WILD CARROTS Serves 4 (v) (V) (GF)

These carrots look so earthy and pretty on the plate, but the key to the presentation of this dish is to leave the greens intact. It's a new, fresh look and flavor for an old, tired side. By not peeling the carrots, you retain more nutrients and also get to be lazy. (Which, of course, is my favorite part.)

INGREDIENTS	METHOD
8 small to medium-sized carrots with greens intact 1 tbsp. fresh dill	Clean carrots well, and don't peel. Carefully slice carrots length-wise once, making sure that a portion of the greens go to each side. Separate carefully. Place about ½ inch water into a large saucepan and bring to a simmer. Place carrot halves into pan, with greens hanging over the edge. Water should not cover carrots completely. Steam carrots until they are only slightly tender (about 5 minutes), and still brightly colored. (Take care the greens don't hang over the pot so far they get singed by the flame!) Transfer to a serving dish and sprinkle with fresh dill. Serve hot.

Curried Grilled Zucchini Serves 4 (v) (V) (GF)

This dish is super easy to cook on any grill, and is especially fabulous if you love to barbeque. The squash is full of flavor, rich in color, and tastes delicious.

Ingredients	Method
2 small zucchinis 1 tbsp. olive oil 1 tbsp. curry powder	Combine oil and curry and whisk until well incorporated. Set aside. Slice zucchini into ⅓-inch rounds. Brush each side with the oil mixture and lay on grill. Grill for 5 minutes on each side. Serve hot.

Mazin' Mashed Potatoes Serves 4 (v) (GF)

These potatoes are a long-time family favorite. You can make them vegan by substituting the cheese for Daiya.

Ingredients	Method
4 large red potatoes, skins intact	Preheat oven to 350 degrees Fahrenheit. Chop potatoes roughly and place in large bowl. Pull rosemary off its stem, rub between your fingers to release flavor, and add to bowl, along with the oil. Mix until potatoes are coated. Place spuds on baking sheet and roast for about 40 minutes, or until tender. Remove from oven, place back into bowl, and mash with skins on. Add onions, cheese, salt, and pepper. Mix well and serve hot.
2 tbsp. olive oil	
1 small sprig rosemary	
¼ cup chopped green onion	
¼ cup finely diced white onion	
¼ cup white sharp cheddar cheese	
Pinch of salt and pepper	

BLISTERED TOMATOES Serves 6 (v) (V) (GF)

These tomatoes are stuffed with the same filling as the Eastern Lettuce Wraps (page 159). If you're not crazy about tomatoes, you can use bell peppers instead.

INGREDIENTS

6 firm field tomatoes

1 portabella mushroom

1 carrot

1 celery stalk

½ white onion, finely diced

3 garlic cloves, minced

1 cup cooked lentils

2 tbsp. gluten-free tamari

1 tbsp. vegan Worcestershire

METHOD

Preheat oven to 350 degrees Fahrenheit. Remove tomato tops and scoop out seeds to form a cavity. Set aside. In food processor, roughly process mushroom, carrots, and celery until they look diced. Set aside. In a large, hot frying pan, brown onion and garlic. Once softened (about 2 minutes), add rest of ingredients. Stir and heat for about 5–7 minutes. Add a little water if you need to, to prevent from burning.

Once mixture is cooked, remove from heat. Scoop about ⅓ cup of mixture into each tomato. Place tomatoes in shallow baking dish and bake for about 20 minutes or until tomatoes begin to slightly blister and are hot. Remove from heat and serve alongside a salad. Enjoy!

Roasted Squash with Apple & Eggplant

Serves 6-8 (v) (V) (GF)

As an alternative to the acorn squash, this recipe is the best way *ever* to use up Halloween pumpkins. Just peel, cube, and freeze them. Then, when you need a warm and delicious side for Thanksgiving or Christmas, break out that frozen pumpkin and make this casserole! (But acorn squash is my fave.)

Ingredients	Method
1 large acorn squash OR 1 small pumpkin	Preheat oven to 350 degrees Fahrenheit. Gut and peel your squash. Cut squash and eggplant into 1-inch cubes and place in bowl. (This should garner about 3 cups, total.) Core and slice apples (don't peel), and add to bowl. Add raisins, cinnamon, and syrup. Mix well, spread into a 9" x 13" casserole dish, and then pour water evenly over top. Sprinkle with Spicy Nuts & Seeds, cover, and bake for 20 minutes.
6 apples	
1 small eggplant	
½ cup raisins	
2 tbsp. cinnamon	
1 tbsp. maple syrup	
½ cup water	Remove cover and bake for another 15 minutes. Remove from oven and enjoy! I like this one hot initially, but leftover and cold is really yummy, too.
1½ cups Spicy Roasted Nuts & Seeds (page 100)	

Steamed Green Salad Serves 4 (v) (V) (GF)

This is a warm salad that will catch your family up on a day's worth of vegetables. The power of herbs is within this dish! It's great for the fall and/or winter, and pairs well with the Blistered Tomatoes (page 113) or Stuffed Portabella Mushrooms (page 118).

Ingredients	Method
½ cup fresh watercress 6 fresh basil leaves ¼ cup fresh dill 2 garlic cloves, minced ¼ cup olive oil 2 tbsp. white wine vinegar 1 tbsp. Dijon mustard 2 tsp. honey 3 large carrots 25 long green beans 1 bunch small asparagus spears	Chop herbs and mix together. Set aside. In a small bowl, whisk together garlic, oil, vinegar, mustard, and honey. Set aside. Cut carrots lengthwise, and steam for 5 minutes in large pot. Add beans and asparagus, and continue steaming together until colors brighten (another 2–3 minutes—don't over-cook!). Remove steamed veggies from heat and drain water. Gently toss in herbs and dressing, mixing evenly. Serve immediately, while still warm.

STUFFED PORTABELLA MUSHROOMS Serves 4 (v) (GF)

This is a great side for its presentation qualities alone! Filling and robust, it's a hearty veggie extra that your omnivorous friends will want to make themselves. It also makes a great entree if you want to double your portion. (Because they're *that* good.) This dish is easily made vegan by substituting the goat cheese or feta for Daiya.

Ingredients	Method
4 portabella mushrooms 1 small fennel bulb ½ yellow onion ½ cup shredded zucchini 2 garlic cloves 2 tbsp. sundried tomatoes 2 tbsp. goat cheese or feta 1 tbsp. avocado oil 1 tbsp. olive oil ¼ cup chopped fresh parsley 1 small sprig fresh rosemary ¼ cup raw pumpkin seeds	Preheat oven to 350 degrees Fahrenheit. Wash mushrooms and pull off stems. Dice mushroom stems, fennel, and onion; shred zucchini; and mince garlic. Place avocado oil in frying pan and heat. Add garlic and onion and heat in pan for about 30 seconds. Add the fennel and mushroom stems, and cook until they are just softened. Remove from heat, and add sundried tomatoes, zucchini, and cheese (if using). Pull the rosemary off its stem and rub between fingers to release flavors. Rip apart and add to mixture. Stir well. Scoop ¼ of mixture into cavity of each mushroom. Brush the sides with olive oil and bake for 20 minutes, or until heated through. Remove from heat, garnish with seeds, parsley, and additional rosemary, and serve alongside a salad or some sprouted brown rice. Yummy!

ROASTED YAMS Serves 4 (v) (V) (GF)

This dish is *so* yummy, and great as a side or on its own. To vary it, try swapping the rosemary for a totally different herb or spice of your choice.

INGREDIENTS	METHOD
1 large yam, peeled and cut into chunks 2 twigs fresh rosemary 2 tbsp. olive oil Pinch of pepper Pinch of salt	Preheat oven to 350 degrees Fahrenheit. Peel the yam, roughly chop, and place in bowl. Pull rosemary off its stem, rub between your fingers to release flavor, and add to bowl. Add oil, pepper, and salt, and mix until yam pieces are evenly coated. Spread evenly on baking sheet in a single layer. Roast for 20 minutes, then flip over and roast for another 20. Serve hot.

Salads have a bad reputation of being boring. Let's change that! The following salad recipes are awesome—nay—*rawsome*. You'll never think salads are uninteresting again. I promise.

Rawsome Salads

GARBANZO QUINOA SALAD Serves 6 (v) GF

This salad is perfect to make for dinner and then bring to work for lunch the next day. It's super high in plant-based protein *and* deliciousness! Garbanzo beans are better known as chickpeas, but I like saying the word "garbanzo," hence the name of this dish. Eliminate the feta to make vegan.

INGREDIENTS	METHOD
1 cup quinoa	Cook quinoa according to package directions, then set aside to cool. Dice cucumber, slice tomatoes in half, and cut basil leaves into thin strips. Drain and rinse beans. In large bowl, combine cooled quinoa, garbanzo beans, cucumbers, tomatoes, basil, and garlic. Add crumbled feta cheese if using. Add Balsamic Vinaigrette, mix together well, and serve. Will keep nicely for a couple of days in the fridge.
½ cucumber	
12 grape tomatoes	
6 basil leaves	
16-oz. can garbanzo beans	
1 tbsp. fresh pressed garlic	
½ cup feta cheese	
¼ cup Balsamic Vinaigrette (page 61)	

SUPERHERO SALAD Serves 2 (v) (V) (GF)

This pretty, summery salad is full of superfoods to fuel the superheroes in your life. If you're looking for something fresh and light, this salad's got your back.

INGREDIENTS	METHOD
1 bunch spinach	Wash and dry spinach, rip into pieces, and plate. Add diced avocado, blueberries, seeds, and nuts. Drizzle dressing to taste.
1 avocado	
½ cup blueberries	
¼ cup pumpkin seeds	
¼ cup walnuts	
Basic Dressing to taste (page 59)	

Sesame Citrus Salad Serves 4 (v) (V) (GF)

This salad is super hearty and fresh, and makes a great spring or summer main dish. The citrus paired with the spinach helps to increase iron absorption, and it seriously hits the spot!

Ingredients

1 small head of frilly green
   cabbage
1 small bunch of spinach
1 medium-sized beet
1 large carrot
1 orange
1 avocado
¼ cup sliced almonds
Spicy Miso Sesame Dressing to
   taste (page 63)

Method

Wash and dry cabbage and spinach. Cut or tear into pieces and place in large bowl. Using a julienne peeler (if you don't have one, then just use a knife), thinly slice beet and carrot into long strips. Add to greens.

Peel orange and section it. Cut sections into halves and add to bowl. Core and peel avocado. Cut into small chunks and add to bowl. Mix veggies well. Garnish with almonds and serve with Spicy Miso Sesame Dressing (page 63).

Rainbow Chard & Beet Salad Serves 2 (v) (GF)

This is a pretty and perfect salad for a fall or winter meal. The warmth of the rice and roasted beet create cozy flavors and textures that make you feel snuggly. Beware: it is a *full* meal—this is no side salad. To make vegan, omit the goat cheese.

Ingredients	Method
8 rainbow chard leaves	Set oven at 350 degrees Fahrenheit. Clean beet and wrap with foil. Place in oven-safe dish and roast for 30–40 minutes, or until tender. Set aside to cool until just warm. Meanwhile, cook rice. Set aside to cool until just warm. Drain and rinse beans.
1 medium-sized beet	
1 cup brown rice	
1 16-oz. can chickpeas	
½ cup raw pecans	
¼ cup raw sunflower seeds	Wash and dry chard, remove spine, and rip leaves into pieces. Divide onto two plates. Dice beets. Divide beets, rice, and chickpeas, and place on top of chard. Add pecans, seeds, and goat cheese. Drizzle dressing on top, and serve immediately.
1 oz. goat cheese	
Balsamic Vinaigrette to taste (page 61)	

WALDORF(ISH) SALAD serves 2 (v) (GF)

I love this salad! Eliminate the blue cheese to make it vegan, and you'll still get that creamy texture from the avocado to create a twist on an old classic. The nuts and seeds give it a little protein boost, and the avocado provides some healthy fat.

Ingredients	Method
1 pear 1 avocado 2 cups arugula 2 tbsp. blue cheese ½ cup Spicy Roasted Nuts & Seeds (page 100) Balsamic Vinaigrette to taste (page 61)	Slice pears thinly and peel, core, and roughly dice avocado. Dividing ingredients in half, plate your lettuce, and arrange pear, avocado, cheese, and Spicy Roasted Nuts & Seeds on top. Drizzle with dressing and enjoy!

TANGY LENTIL SALAD **Serves 2 (v) (V) (GF)**

I'm absolutely wild about this salad! It's super high in fiber and protein and has a nice, lemony finish. It tastes great on its own or as a side dish. It also keeps well for a couple of days, so if you want, you can make enough to bring to work the next day.

INGREDIENTS

½ small red onion

1 cup grape tomatoes

¼ cup flat-leaf parsley

1 16-oz. can lentils

½ small lemon

2 tbsp. seedy mustard

4 tbsp. extra virgin olive oil

½ tsp. sea salt

Cracked pepper to taste

METHOD

Dice the onion, slice tomatoes in half, and chop parsley. Place in large bowl. Drain and rinse lentils well, then place in bowl with veggies and set aside.

Squeeze the juice from half the lemon into a small bowl and add mustard, oil, and salt. Whisk together until smooth and well-incorporated. Pour over lentil mixture and stir well. Serve with some cracked pepper over top. Enjoy!

Green Salad with Tofu Serves 2 (v) (V) (GF)

This is a light salad, but it still packs some heavy protein. It's also a great way to practice cooking tofu!

Ingredients

½ package of organic, firm tofu

1 tsp. sea salt

1 small head leaf lettuce

½ cup bean sprouts

½ cucumber

¼ cup pumpkin seeds

¼ cup Oriental Dressing (page 64)

Method (for tofu)

Remove the tofu from its packaging and divide in half. Slice into rectangles about half an inch thick. Once your half block of tofu is sliced, place the pieces in an 8" x 8" baking dish in a single layer. Combine about 1 cup of warm water with salt and pour over tofu until all rectangles are fully immersed. Soak for about fifteen minutes.

Place tofu on top of a double layer of paper towel and then cover with another double layer. Gently press, until all of the water is out. You might have to repeat this step twice.

Get your pan hot (I use cast iron for this) and add 1 tbsp. coconut oil in the pan to grease it. Place tofu in pan in a single layer. Cook for about 3–4 minutes on each side, until both sides of the tofu rectangles are browned. Sprinkle with sea salt and set aside.

Method (for salad)

Wash and dry your lettuce. Rip into bite-size pieces and arrange on plate. Add clean sprouts. Wash your cucumber and slice lengthwise. Slice again into half-moons and arrange over lettuce, then sprinkle on seeds. Arrange tofu directly on top and drizzle dressing over the salad. Enjoy immediately!

Seeds & Stuff Salad Serves 4 (v) (V) (GF)

This salad feels like a big meal, and as the name suggests, it has a lot of stuff!

Ingredients

1 bunch leaf lettuce

1 cup red and yellow firm grape
tomatoes

½ cucumber

½ cup sprouted mung beans

½ cup spouts (any kind)

¼ cup raw sunflower seeds

¼ cup pumpkin seeds

¼ cup raisins

1 avocado, diced into chunks

Dill Dressing to taste (page 62)

Method

Wash and dry lettuce, then tear into pieces and place in large bowl. Slice tomatoes in half and set aside. Slice cucumber in half, then half again lengthwise, then horizontally to make half-moons. Add sprouted mung beans, garlic sprouts, tomatoes, cucumber, seeds, and raisins to bowl. Toss well. Divide salad into four dishes, top with avocado, and drizzle Dill Dressing to taste. Enjoy!

Spinach & Strawberry Salad serves 2 (v) (GF)

This salad is so pretty and light—a perfect summer meal. To make vegan, omit the goat cheese.

Ingredients	Method
4 cups fresh baby spinach	Divide spinach into two bowls. Wash, dry, and hull the strawberries. Slice the berries into quarters and slice onion into strips. Add to spinach, along with the chickpeas. Divide goat cheese and crumble over salads. In small bowl, whisk together the mustard, vinegar, oil, honey, and garlic. Roll sage with fingers to release the flavor and fragrance. Chop into tiny pieces and add to dressing mixture. Finish this gem off by drizzling dressing over top the salads, taking care not to over-season. Bon appétit!
6 strawberries	
¼ red onion	
½ cup drained and rinsed chick-peas	
1 tbsp. goat cheese	
½ tbsp. Dijon mustard	
1 tbsp. balsamic vinegar	
1½ tbsp. olive oil	
½ tbsp. honey	
1 garlic clove, minced	
2 sage leaves	

"If diet is wrong, medicine is of no use. If diet
is correct, medicine is of no need."[12]
–Ancient Ayurvedic proverb

All of the following recipes are *so* yummy. They're also (for the most part) super easy, and pretty quick to throw together. I absolutely *loathe* recipes that are complicated and take forever, so I promise, I would never do that to you. Now let's get cooking! (And by "let's," I mean *you*.)

Main Eats

GREEN SPAGHETTI Serves 4 (v)

This pasta dish is light, but heavy on the greens. If desired, omit the Parmesan cheese for a fully vegan meal, and a genuinely guilt-free pasta.

INGREDIENTS	METHOD

1 bunch asparagus
Enough whole wheat spaghetti
    noodles to serve 4
1 bunch raw spinach
½ cup pine nuts, divided
2 cloves of garlic
1 tbsp. lemon juice
1 avocado, pitted, skinned, and
    diced
Small block Parmesan cheese
	Steam asparagus in pot until bright green, about 2 minutes. (Don't overcook!) Remove from pot. Using the asparagus water (adding some fresh water to the pot if needed), bring to a boil and add pasta to cook.
	
	Meanwhile, combine spinach, asparagus, ¼ cup of nuts, garlic, and lemon juice in food processor. Process until it becomes a slightly chunky, but mostly creamy consistency. If needed, add a little water.
	
	Drain pasta, rinse with hot water, and toss with green sauce from processor. Divide into four and top with avocado and remaining pine nuts. Grate fresh Parmesan cheese over top. Bon appétit!

BLACK BEAN TACOS WITH SLAW Serves 3 (v) (V) (GF)

This is one of my favorite dinner meals. I love messy eats, and this one is up there with the best of them. Go ahead—try and make them only once. *I dare you.* Note: Fresh Salsa (page 94) already contains black beans, but for this dish you will want to add extra. Hence the additional cup of beans, and the name of this dish. Bean it up!

Ingredients	Method
1 cup drained and rinsed black beans	Combine black beans, salsa, and chili powder in one bowl, mixing well. Set aside. Toss together cabbage, oil, lime juice, seeds, and avocado in another bowl.
1 cup Fresh Salsa (page 94)	
2 tbsp. chili powder	Fill your corn shell half way with the bean mixture and top with the cabbage mixture. Grab a napkin, and dig in!
¼ cup raw sunflower seeds	
1 avocado, diced	
6 hard taco shells (organic, corn)	
½ small head of chopped raw cabbage	
2 tbsp. avocado oil	
Juice of 1 lime	

EGGPLANT LASAGNE Serves 6 (v)

This hearty lasagne is major comfort food, and super flavorful. The chia seeds act as a binding agent in place of egg, but if you aren't concerned with this dish being completely plant-based, then you can just go ahead and substitute the chia seeds for one free-range egg. If you want a completely vegan dish, keep the chia seeds, and replace the mozzarella cheese with Daiya.

INGREDIENTS	METHOD
1 onion	Set oven at 350 degrees Fahrenheit and wash all produce. Combine onion, carrots, celery, and mushrooms in your food processor. Process on high for about 5 seconds. Combine veggie mixture with diced tomatoes, flaxseed, and all spices in stainless steel pot. Cover and simmer for 30 minutes.
2 carrots	
4 celery stalks	
1 cup mushrooms	
4 cups diced tomatoes in juices	
¼ cup ground flaxseed	
1 tbsp. onion powder	Meanwhile, cook noodles until half done (al dente—still firm). Thinly slice eggplant lengthwise about 8 times. Sparingly coat 9" x 13" baking dish with avocado oil. Beginning with the noodles, cover the bottom in a single layer. Stir chia seeds into sauce, mixing well, and spoon ⅓ of the sauce over the noodles. Lay eggplant in single layer over top, and then cover generously with spinach.
4 garlic cloves	
1 tbsp. oregano	
1 tbsp. red chili pepper flakes	
1 package whole wheat lasagne noodles	
1 small eggplant	Repeat with noodles, sauce, eggplant, spinach, noodles, and then end with sauce. Sprinkle with Mozzarella and bake for 45 minutes. Let cool for 15 minutes before cutting and serving.
2 tbsp. avocado oil	
¼ cup chia seeds	
1 bunch spinach	
1 cup Mozzarella cheese	

Marie's Thai Curry Serves 4 (v) (V) (GF)

This Thai dish is to die for. It's completely vegan, and totally amazing. A fabulous meal to share with friends or eat as leftovers alone in a dark corner while your neighbors pound on the door begging to find out where that scrumptious smell is coming from. (True story.) I totally recommend serving over brown, sprouted rice.

Ingredients	Method
1 yellow onion	Dice onion and potatoes, mince garlic, cut pepper into long, thin strips, break apart cauliflower into bite-size pieces, and cut tofu into one-inch cubes. Set aside.
3 yellow potatoes	
3 garlic cloves	
1 large red bell pepper	Spoon out half of one of the cans of coconut milk (incorporating any thicker part) and bring to a gentle boil over medium heat. Cook, stirring occasionally, until milk releases its sweet fragrance (about three minutes). Add curry and cayenne and cook for three minutes more, stirring often to combine it with the coconut milk.
1 bunch cauliflower florets	
1 package firm tofu	
2 cans unsweetened, full-fat coconut milk	
2 tbsp. yellow curry powder	Add onion and garlic, stirring gently to coat with curry mixture. Sauté for 5 minutes. Add remaining 1½ cans coconut milk, tofu, potatoes, cauliflower, and bamboo shoots. Combine well and bring to an active boil. Reduce heat and maintain a simmer for 15 minutes, stirring occasionally.
1 tsp. cayenne pepper	
½ cup bamboo shoots	
	Add bell pepper strips and stir gently. Cook for 5 more minutes, until peppers are cooked but not too soft. Serve over brown rice.
	*Many thanks to Marie Arnold for this contribution.

YAM BURGER Serves 4 (v) (V) (GF)

This totally vegan burger is super delish and full of fiber. It's also really messy, so I suggest being prepared with napkins. (I know—this is becoming a fairly common warning. I never said I wasn't a mess . . . uhhh . . . I mean the burger . . . the *burger's* a mess . . .)

Ingredients	Method
1 large yam	Preheat oven to 350 degrees Fahrenheit. Peel, chop, and roast your yam on a baking sheet for about 30 minutes, or until tender. Remove from oven and combine yams, quinoa, lentils, chili powder, and salt in large bowl. Mash together roughly until well combined but still chunky. Add oats, mix well, cover, and refrigerate for one hour.
½ cup cooked quinoa	
½ cup drained and rinsed lentils	
1 tsp. chili powder	
½ tsp. sea salt	
⅓ cup gluten-free rolled oats	
8 large pieces leaf lettuce	Meanwhile, wash remaining produce, dry leaves, and slice tomatoes and peppers thinly. Once burger mixture is ready, heat oil in skillet on medium heat. Separate burger mixture into four parts, and shape into patties. Drop onto the oil and cook for about 5 minutes on each side, until golden and slightly crusty on outside.
2 Roma tomatoes	
1 yellow, red, or orange bell pepper	
2 tbsp. avocado oil	
1 cup Karley's Famous Guacamole (page 99) (optional)	To assemble burgers, lay one piece of lettuce on plate, top with tomato and pepper slices, ¼ cup of Karley's Famous Guacamole, a yam patty, and then another piece of lettuce over top. Make sure you have a napkin, and enjoy! Goes well with a side garden salad.

EASY AS (PIZZA) PIE Serves 2 (v)

This pizza is super simple to make, and has a very low calorie density. It pairs well with a salad on the side. If you'd prefer a completely vegan pizza, go ahead and substitute the cheese for Daiya—it's just as delish. Note: keep in mind that some veggies have more protein than others. For example, mushrooms have lots! So if you are interested in increasing your protein intake, throw some 'shrooms on your pizza!

Ingredients	Method
2 large whole grain tortillas	Preheat oven to 400 degrees Fahrenheit. Place tortillas on cookie sheets or pizza pans. Brush with tomato sauce, top with veggies, and drop small amounts of cheese on top. Rub basil leaves lightly between your fingers and thumb, then place on top.
¼ cup prepared organic tomato sauce	
Any assortment of any fresh veggies you like	
½ cup gorgonzola cheese	Bake for 6–8 minutes, until wraps become crunchy around the edges. Cut into halves, then quarters. Place two pieces on each plate, surround with salad, and consume immediately!
Handful of fresh basil leaves	

Lazy Cabbage Roll Casserole   Serves 4 (v) (V) (GF)

This cool-weather dish is a super easy way to make vegan cabbage rolls. ('Cuz there's no rolling involved.) It's fantastic as leftovers, too—in fact, it might be better.

Ingredients

1½ cups brown rice

1 tbsp. sesame oil

1 white onion

2 garlic cloves

1 16-oz. can crushed tomatoes

1 jar prepared tomato sauce
  (25 oz.)

1 package vegan ground round

2 tbsp. vegan Worcestershire

1 head green cabbage, roughly
  cut into bite-size pieces

Method

Cook your rice according to package directions and set aside. Preheat oven to 350 degrees Fahrenheit. Place saucepan over medium heat and add oil. Chop onion and mince garlic, then add to saucepan and cook for about 2 minutes. Add crushed tomatoes, tomato sauce, ground round, cooked rice, and Worcestershire. Mix well and simmer for 10 minutes.

Meanwhile, tear or cut up cabbage. In an 8" x 8" baking dish, layer cabbage, and then sauce mixture. Repeat. Cover and cook for 30 minutes. Remove cover and cook for another 15 minutes. Remove from oven and let sit for 15 minutes before serving hot. Add a little bit of salt and pepper to taste, just before eating.

Red Lentil Soup Serves 6 (v) (V) (GF)

My neighbor makes this soup, and I can smell it from inside my house. I've literally knocked on his door, empty bowl in hand, he's filled it for me, and then I've walked back home to eat it. It's ridiculously amazing. (And yeah—I'm *that* neighbor.)

Ingredients

2 cups dried red lentils

3 cloves garlic

2 medium onions

2 stalks celery

2 carrots

4 tbsp. tomato paste

½ cup olive oil

½ tsp. black pepper

8 cups water

2 tsp. salt

¼ cup red wine vinegar

Dash of your favorite hot sauce
  (optional)

Method

Rinse and sort (remove any dark or broken) lentils and place in large pot. Mince the garlic and dice the onions, celery, and carrots. Add to pot, along with the rest of the ingredients, except the red wine vinegar. Cover and bring to a boil, reduce heat, and simmer for about 1½ hours. Stir in red wine vinegar and serve.

*Thanks to Andreas Kammenos for this contribution.

SQUASHED PUTTANESCA   Serves 2 (v) (V) (GF)

This gorgeously healthy dinner will satisfy the Italian in you. Who needs pasta? Not I! I have never made this when it was *not* been a total score. It's super high in fiber and is fabulously flavorful.

INGREDIENTS

1 spaghetti squash

4 tbsp. olive oil

1 small white onion

2 garlic cloves

1 small fennel bulb

3 cooked artichoke hearts

1 16-oz. can of crushed tomatoes

1 tbsp. capers

½ cup sliced black olives

½ cup fresh, chopped parsley

METHOD

Preheat oven to 350 degrees Fahrenheit. Cut squash lengthwise into two halves. Grease cookie sheet with half the oil and place squash flat-side down on sheet. Bake for 40 minutes. Meanwhile, dice the onion, mince the garlic, slice fennel into "v" shapes, and quarter your artichokes.

Place pot on stove and heat on medium. Once hot, add remaining oil and throw in onion and garlic. Let them brown while pushing around with spatula for about 2 minutes. Add tomatoes and fennel. Cover and simmer for about 15 minutes. Then remove cover and add artichokes, capers, and olives, and simmer for another 5 minutes.

Remove squash from oven and flip over. Set two plates close to stove. Remove the middle stringy, seedy part of the squash using a large spoon. Using a fork, scrape the cavity of the squash so that it comes out in strips, like spaghetti.

Once squash is plated, it should resemble spaghetti noodles. Top with sauce and then garnish with chopped parsley. Enjoy immensely, and then immediately find my blog and thank me publicly. *You're welcome.*

GRILLED BEAN & GREEN QUESADILLA Serves 2 (v)

This is truly one green quesadilla. Substitute the cheese for Daiya if you'd prefer this dish to be vegan.

INGREDIENTS

2 large whole grain tortillas

¼ cup Perfect Pesto (page 67)

1 cup spinach

½ zucchini

½ green pepper

½ cup cilantro

1 16-oz. can black beans

1 cup shredded Monterey Jack cheese

1 cup Karley's Famous Guacamole (page 99)

METHOD

Lay tortilla shells flat on counter. Spread each tortilla with half of the Perfect Pesto. Slice zucchini and pepper and chop the cilantro. Drain and rinse beans. Layer greens and beans on one half of the shells. Sprinkle ¼ cup of cheese on top and carefully fold over empty half of tortilla shell. (It will look huge, but with shrink once the veggies heat up.)

Heat grill. Once hot, place quesadillas directly on the grill. Cook for about 2 minutes, then carefully flip quesadillas over to cook other side for another 2 minutes. Once shells are crispy and show grill lines, remove, plate, and cut quesadillas into thirds. Top each with a half cup of Karley's Famous Guacamole. Olé!

LENTIL LOAF Makes 2 loaves (v) (V) (GF)

My husband and I both love this healthy version of meat loaf. It tastes like the real thing, only better. The longer you let it sit after cooking, the better it firms up. If you're in a hurry, it might be a little crumbly, but it tastes amazing. (I can never wait. I've also been known to crunch hard candy, which drives my husband nuts. Patience is not my thing.)

INGREDIENTS

1½ tbsp. avocado oil

6 mushrooms

3 celery stalks

½ white onion

¼ cup fresh parsley

3 cloves garlic

1 cup firm tofu

1 16-oz. can lentils

1 cup gluten-free rolled oats

3 tbsp. tomato sauce

3 tbsp. tamari

1 tbsp. chia seeds

Salt and pepper to taste

½ cup pumpkin seeds

METHOD

Preheat oven to 350 degrees and grease your loaf pan with ½ tablespoon of oil. Finely chop mushrooms, celery, onion, and parsley. Mince garlic. Place remaining oil in frying pan and add veggies and minced garlic. Sauté for about 4–5 minutes, or until soft. Place in large mixing bowl.

Next, crumble tofu and add to bowl with sautéed vegetables. Add lentils, oats, parsley, tomato sauce, tamari, chia seeds, salt, and pepper. Mix well. Once the mixture is the right texture (you should be able to form into balls if desired), place in greased loaf pan. Sprinkle with pumpkin seeds and bake for about 45 minutes, or until crust is browned.

Remove from oven and let cool for 10 minutes before slicing to serve. Serve with Wild Carrots (page 109) and Mazin' Mashed Potatoes (page 111). Enjoy!

Sweet & Sour Tofu Stir-Fry Serves 4 (v) (V) (GF)

This recipe is restaurant-style, and absolutely does not disappoint. Use it to convince even the most carnivorous of meat eaters that vegan cooking is incredible. My husband's not the hugest tofu fan, but he *loves* this one.

Ingredients

2 cups brown rice

1 small white onion

2 garlic cloves

1 carrot

1 small thumb of ginger, peeled

1 package firm tofu

1 tbsp. coconut oil

1 cup fresh pineapple chunks

⅓ cup orange or pineapple juice

2 tbsp. gluten-free tamari

1 tbsp. rice vinegar

1 tbsp. sesame seeds

Method

Cook rice according to package directions and set aside. Chop the onion, mince the garlic, julienne the carrot, grate the ginger, and cut tofu into even chunks.

Heat oil in large frying pan and add onions and garlic. Sauté for 3–4 minutes, until fragrant. Add carrots and ginger and stir-fry for another 3–4 minutes. Add tofu and stir-fry until it begins to brown (about 10 minutes). Add pineapple, juice, tamari, and vinegar.

Cover and cook for another 5–7 minutes. Serve hot over brown rice and drizzle a little extra tamari on there, if you'd like. Garnish with sesame seeds.

EASTERN LETTUCE WRAPS Serves 4 (v) (V) (GF)

These wraps are incredible. They're high in protein, fiber, and general awesomeness. To make truly vegetarian or vegan, be sure to use vegan Worcestershire. (Traditional Worcestershire has fish sauce in it.)

Ingredients	Method
1 head of romaine lettuce	Separate lettuce leaves, wash and dry, and set aside. In food processor, roughly process mushroom, carrots, and celery until they're diced. Set aside. Dice the onion and mince garlic. Drain and rinse the beans.
1 portabella mushroom	
1 carrot	
1 celery stalk	
½ white onion	Heat frying pan and add oil, and then add onions and garlic. Once softened (about 3 minutes), add rest of vegetables, lentils, tamari, and Worcestershire. Heat mixture for about 10 minutes while stirring every now and then. (Add a little water if you need to.)
3 garlic cloves	
1 tbsp. sesame oil	
1 16-oz. can lentils	
2 tbsp. gluten-free tamari	Once mixture is heated through, remove from heat. Using 2 open leaves per person, scoop about ½ cup of mixture into each leaf. Roll up and eat immediately!
1 tbsp. vegan Worcestershire	

VEGALICIOUS CHILI Serves 6 (v) (V) (GF)

My husband prefers this dish without the vegan ground round, but I prefer it with. Your choice! It's perfect for a cool autumn day, and especially if you're in the mood for something hearty. Also—and this is my favorite part—it's great for leftovers *and* it freezes well!

INGREDIENTS

1 16-oz. can red kidney beans

1 yellow onion

1 green pepper

2 carrots

2 cloves garlic

3 mushrooms

3 cups diced tomatoes

1 cup water

1 tbsp. chili powder

1 tsp. red pepper chili flakes

1 tsp. onion powder

¼ tsp. garlic salt

2 bay leaves

1 package vegan ground round
  (optional)

METHOD

Drain and rinse beans well, then set aside. Combine onion, green pepper, carrots, and garlic in food processor. Process for about 7–8 seconds on high, then slice your mushrooms. Combine veggie mixture with mushrooms, beans, tomatoes, water, spices, and bay leaves in crockpot. Cook on high for two hours, or low for 6 hours, stirring occasionally.

Just before serving, break up ground round and stir into chili. Let chili sit (to allow ground round to heat up) for about 5 minutes. Remove bay leaves and serve hot.

Those who know me well know that there's no way my dessert section of a cookbook could be anything but the largest section. I can't help it—I love the sweet stuff! Here are more than a dozen delicious concoctions that will satisfy your sweet tooth, while keeping with the theme of whole, plant-based foods. These recipes make me happy, and I hope they make you happy, too.

Sweet Tooth

Pink Salt Two-Bite Brownies

Makes about 2 dozen (v) (V) (GF)

These raw, vegan goodies take only about 10 minutes to make, a few hours to set, and they taste *divine*. Note: If you'd like these a little sweeter, substitute the cacao nibs for dark chocolate chips.

Ingredients	Method
1½ cups walnuts ½ cup raw cocoa powder ½ tbsp. coarse pink Himalayan sea salt ½ tsp. cinnamon 1 cup dried, pitted dates 4 tbsp. hot water 2 tbsp. raw, sweetened cacao nibs	Add walnuts to your food processor and pulse on low until they are in small pieces. Add cacao powder, half of the sea salt, and cinnamon. Pulse until well combined. Next add the dates, about four at a time, until they're well incorporated. Add water and blend thoroughly. Your mixture will look slightly chunky. Lastly, add the nibs and pulse a few times. Line a mini-muffin pan and scoop batter into liners. Using your fingers, press gently until they're firm. Sprinkle rest of sea salt on top of your brownies, refrigerate overnight to set, and enjoy in the morning! (*Ahem—I mean *after dinner*.) Store in airtight container for up to a week.

FIGGY FRUIT PARFAIT Makes 1 serving (v) (GF)

This could easily double as a breakfast food, but I love it as a snack or a post-workout munch. The figs and dates are naturally sweet, and easily satisfy any sugary craving I may be experiencing. To make vegan, substitute the Greek yogurt for the organic soy variety.

INGREDIENTS	METHOD
1 apple	Slice apple thinly and quarter figs and plums. Zest your orange until you have about a teaspoon's worth and chop the dates. Layer apple slices, fig, plum, dates, walnuts, yogurt, and orange zest in that order. Eat immediately!
1 ripe fig	
1 ripe plum	
1 small orange	
2 pitted dates	
5 raw walnuts	
½ cup organic, plain Greek yogurt	

CRISPY CHOCOLATE PEANUT BUTTER BARS

Makes 16 bars (v) (V) (GF)

These guys are a twist on the conventional Rice Krispy Square—sans gelatin and way too much processed sugar. Brown rice syrup is much lower on the glycemic index than other liquid sweeteners; these babies are smooth, delicious, and not overly sweet. If you want to get creative, you can melt some dark chocolate to drizzle over the bars before placing them in the refrigerator. I'm drooling already . . .

INGREDIENTS	METHOD
4 cups crispy brown rice cereal	Measure out cereal, place in large bowl, and set aside. Combine rest of ingredients in saucepan and heat over medium. Stir constantly until well combined and beginning to bubble. Remove from heat and pour into bowl over cereal. Mix well and pour into an 8" x 8" baking pan. Press down flat with your hands until firm and uniform and refrigerate for 1–2 hours. Cut into 16 bars and serve.
¾ cup natural peanut butter	
¾ cup brown rice syrup	
2 tbsp. unsweetened cocoa powder	
3 tbsp. white chia seeds	

Chocolate-Pumpkin Loaf Makes 1 loaf (v)

This bread is dense and decadent—you can actually use this batter for cookies, too!

Ingredients	Method
¼ cup applesauce	Boil some water in a tea kettle, preheat oven to 350 degrees Fahrenheit, and line a loaf pan with parchment paper.
2 tbsp. coconut oil	
⅓ cup unsweetened cocoa powder	Place applesauce, coconut oil, and cocoa powder in a mixing bowl and mix well. Measure out ½ cup of hot water, and pour *most* of it (reserve a couple of tablespoons) into the bowl with the chocolate mixture, mixing quickly to make a smooth chocolate sauce. Add pumpkin, sugar, and vanilla, mixing well. Set aside.
½ cup hot water, divided	
1 cup organic pumpkin puree	
½ cup organic, raw cane sugar	
1 tsp. pure vanilla extract	
1½ cups whole wheat flour	Sift together flour, spices, salt, and baking soda. Combine half the flour mixture with the chocolate mixture, along with the remainder of the hot water, and stir. Add the rest of the flour mixture and the other tablespoon of boiling water to the chocolate mixture and stir until smooth. Add chocolate chips and mix again, just until chocolate chips are incorporated.
½ tsp. ground cinnamon	
¼ tsp. ground nutmeg	
¼ tsp. ground ginger	
⅛ tsp. ground cloves	
¾ tsp. salt	
¾ tsp. baking soda	
¼ cup dark chocolate chips	
¼ cup raw pumpkin seeds	Spoon the batter into the prepared loaf pan. It will be smooth and thick and look more like cookie dough. Sprinkle with seeds, bake for one hour, and let cool for about 10–15 minutes before removing from pan. Slice and serve!

Banana-Oat Cookies

Makes about 2 dozen cookies (v) (V) (GF)

These suckers are easy, wholesome, and are made with only 5 ingredients (the coconut oil doesn't count). I dare you not to eat them all immediately, but if you do, you wouldn't be the first.

Ingredients	Method
1 tbsp. coconut oil	Preheat oven to 375 degrees Fahrenheit and grease cookie sheet with oil. In large bowl, mash bananas. Add rest of ingredients, mix together, then drop by spoonfuls onto cookie sheet and flatten slightly with your palm. Bake for about 12–14 minutes, then let set for 2 minutes on cookie sheet before removing to cooling rack. Enjoy!
3 ripe bananas	
2 cups gluten-free rolled oats	
½ cup unsweetened, shredded coconut	
½ cup raisins or chopped dates	
3 tbsp. chia seeds	

PURPLE BERRY CRUMBLE Serves 8 (v) (V) (GF)

This treat tastes great topped with coconut milk ice cream or full-fat Greek yogurt. It's a hit every single time.

INGREDIENTS

6 cups fresh or frozen berries

¼ cup raw cane sugar

½ cup unsweetened coconut spread

½ cup brown rice syrup

2 cups gluten-free rolled oats

½ cup brown rice flour

METHOD

Preheat oven to 350 degrees Fahrenheit. Combine berries and sugar in a 9" x 13" baking pan. In a bowl, mix together rest of ingredients, mashing until well incorporated. Sprinkle over fruit and press down slightly with fingers to create a crust. Bake, uncovered, for 50 minutes, or until bubbly. Serve warm or cold!

CHUNKY MONKEY COOKIES Makes 2 dozen (v) (GF)

These cookies are soft and fabulous and entirely flourless. Be careful—they vanish quickly. (And, ummm . . . *so does the batter*.) They're nutritious enough to eat for breakfast, and I'm not just saying that to make myself feel better; although if you ate them for breakfast, it might do just that. To make vegan, substitute the chocolate chips for cacao nibs.

INGREDIENTS	METHOD
3 ripe bananas	Preheat oven to 350 degrees Fahrenheit. Mash bananas in a large bowl and then stir in remaining ingredients. Let batter stand for about 10 minutes (this is important—it's how the batter thickens up). Drop by small spoonfuls onto ungreased cookie sheet and flatten slightly with a fork. Bake for 12 minutes. Let cool completely, and then enjoy!
2½ cups gluten-free rolled oats	
¼ cup almond butter	
¼ cup unsweetened cocoa powder	
⅓ cup unsweetened applesauce	
½ cup dark chocolate chips	
¼ cup chia seeds	
1 tsp. vanilla extract	

ENERGY BARS Makes 16 bars (v) (V) (GF)

These bars make perfect companions when traveling, a post-workout snack, or when you're stuck in a business meeting that just . . . won't . . . end. Make them a day ahead and take with you everywhere for fast energy and a happy tummy.

Ingredients	Method
1½ cups gluten-free rolled oats	Line an 8" x 8" baking pan with parchment paper and set aside. Combine all ingredients and mix well until sticky and evenly coated. If mixture is too dry, add a bit of warm water. Pour mixture into pan and pat down firmly. Cover with foil and refrigerate overnight. In the morning, cut into bars and either keep in the pan or wrap individually with foil. Enjoy!
¼ cup pumpkin seeds	
¼ cup dried cranberries	
¼ cup sunflower seeds	
½ cup almond butter	
¼ cup walnut pieces	
2 tbsp. chia seeds	
2 tbsp. flax seeds	
½ cup brown rice syrup	

Dark Chocolate Bars with Himalayan Sea Salt

Makes about 2 dozen pieces (v) (GF)

These are sweet and salty and very pretty. If you're making this for a holiday treat, you can add 2 tsp. of peppermint extract to the chocolate, swap the almonds for pistachio nuts, and skip the salt.

Ingredients	Method
½ cup raw almonds 16-oz. block of dark chocolate ½ tsp. coarse pink Himalayan sea salt	Line a 9" x 13" baking pan with parchment paper. Chop the almonds into small pieces and set aside. Melt chocolate in a double boiler, stirring continuously. Once melted, stir almonds into chocolate and pour into lined pan. Gripping pan with both hands, try and even out the chocolate as best as you can until it appears smooth. Sprinkle salt evenly over the chocolate, then refrigerate overnight. To remove from pan, pull out the parchment paper and remove the block of set chocolate. Break into pieces and enjoy! Keep refrigerated.

SUGAR-FREE APPLE CRISP Serves 8 (v) (GF)

This recipe is perfect for those looking to consume less sugar but who have a non-cooperative sweet tooth. That tooth won't know what hit it! Substitute the butter for Earth's Balance Buttery Spread if you'd like a completely vegan crisp.

INGREDIENTS	METHOD
12 ripe golden delicious apples	Preheat oven to 350 degrees Fahrenheit. Leaving the peels on, core and slice apples. Place in bowl and add cloves and half the cinnamon. Mix well and pour into a 9" x 13" baking dish. Set aside.
1 tsp. cloves	
1 tbsp. cinnamon	
2 cups gluten-free rolled oats	
½ cup quinoa flour	Mix the rest of the ingredients together in bowl and pour over apple mixture. Spread evenly and pat down (don't worry about any lasting clumps of butter—it's all good). Cover with foil and bake for 30 minutes, then remove foil and bake for another 15 minutes. Once cooked, let sit for 10 minutes and then serve warm or cold—it's delicious both ways!
2 tbsp. organic butter	
½ cup unsweetened applesauce	

Homemade Applesauce with Spicy Roasted Nuts & Seeds Serves 4 (v) (V) (GF)

I have a little apple tree in my backyard that produces really ugly apples. But I make them into applesauce and everyone loves them. Spotty, disfigured apples need love, too!

Ingredients	Method
12 apples 1 tbsp. cinnamon 1 cup water 2 cups Spicy Roasted Nuts & Seeds (page 100)	Core and quarter your apples. (You don't have to peel them, and it's actually healthier if you don't, but I peel the ones from my tree because their peels aren't pretty.) Place in large pot on stove over medium-low heat with cinnamon and water. Stir occasionally over the course of about 45 minutes to an hour. Once apples are all soft and easily stirred, it's up to you to decide when they're done. Personally, I prefer slightly chunky applesauce, but cook them until you think the applesauce looks good. Remove from heat and let cool for twenty minutes, stirring occasionally. Dollop into four dishes and serve warm topped with Spicy Roasted Nuts and Seeds. Enjoy!

POACHED PEARS Serves 6 (v) (GF)

This warm dessert is so yummy, especially in the winter. My kids go crazy for it! If you want it totally vegan, substitute the Greek yogurt for soy yogurt or coconut milk "ice cream."

INGREDIENTS

3 pears (not overly ripe)

½ tbsp. raw cane sugar

1 tbsp. cinnamon

¼ tsp. cloves

1¼ cups Greek yogurt

¾ cup Spicy Roasted Nuts & Seeds (page 100)

METHOD

Preheat oven to 350 degrees Fahrenheit. Core pears and cut in half. Place a small amount of water into a 9" x 13" baking pan, so that it's about ¼ inch deep. Place pears skin-side down (flesh-side up) in baking pan.

Combine sugar, cinnamon, and cloves. Divide evenly and sprinkle mixture over each pear. Bake for 30–40 minutes until tender. Turn oven to broil and cook pears for another 2–3 minutes, or until tops begin to brown. (Keep an eye on these guys—the sugar burns fast!)

Remove from oven, fill each cavity with 3 tablespoons of yogurt, and sprinkle 2 tablespoons of Roasted Nuts & Seeds over each pear half. Serve immediately.

CHOCOLATE CHIA PUDDING Makes 1 serving (v) (V) (GF)

A great friend of mine got me hooked on this one. It makes a yummy snack, and even the kids like it. (Which is a victory in itself.)

INGREDIENTS	METHOD
1 cup organic chocolate soy milk 3 tbsp. chia seeds 1 tbsp. raw coconut flakes	Stir chia seeds into milk, on and off, for about five minutes. (Seeds need to be evenly distributed in the milk—this is important so that it sets properly.) Cover and refrigerate overnight. In the morning, sprinkle coconut on top and eat right away. High-fiber pudding for breakfast! Or leave refrigerated and add coconut flakes just before serving.

APRICOT BARS Makes 6 bars (v) (V) (GF)

These bars are another product of the mighty food processor! They taste like thick homemade fruit leather, but are full of protein and fiber. Try to use dried apricots from a sealed bag. The ones in the bulk bins are usually too dried out, and then the bars don't stick together as well. If this is the case, you can soak the apricots in some warm water for five minutes and then drain before using. In this recipe, sticky is *key*.

INGREDIENTS	METHOD
1½ cups dried apricots ⅓ cup raw walnuts ¼ cup unsweetened coconut, divided 1 tsp. white chia seeds ¼ cup hot water Pecans and pumpkin seeds to garnish	Line loaf pan with parchment paper. Combine all ingredients (except for half the coconut) in food processor and blend on high for about 1 minute until well-ground and sticky. Place mixture into pan and spread evenly. Top with remaining 2 tbsp. of coconut. Press mixture down firmly with your fingers so that bars stick together well and are dense. Decorate with nuts and seeds if you want, then refrigerate overnight. The next day, cut into six bars. Store in fridge in an airtight container for up to a week.

Coconut Bliss Balls

Makes approximately 36 balls (v) (V) (GF)

The original name for this recipe was "Nut Balls," but I got *very* made fun of for it. Coconut Bliss Balls sounds a little better, I guess. (Not as much fun, though.)

Ingredients	Method
2 cups pitted dates	Mix all ingredients except for coconut together in food processor until well combined. Form into balls, roll in coconut, and place on parchment paper or in mini muffin cups as you go. Store in mini muffin cups in an airtight container in the refrigerator for up to 2 weeks.
½ cup warm water	
¾ cup gluten-free rolled oats	
¼ cup sesame seeds	
¼ cup sunflower seeds	
¼ cup salted pumpkin seeds	
¼ cup chopped almonds	
¼ cup cranberries	
½ cup unsweetened shredded coconut	

Dark Chocolate Chip Cookies Makes about 2 dozen cookies (v) (GF)

These little cookies are crazy good! They are vegan, gluten-free, can be raw if you don't want to bake them, and can be made completely kosher, too! Play with the ingredients if you can think of more yummy things to throw in, such as swapping the chocolate chips for raisins.

Ingredients	Method
2 cups raw walnuts 15 pitted dates ¼ cup gluten-free rolled oats ¼ cup shredded coconut ½ cup water ¼ cup dark chocolate chips 1 tbsp. ground flaxseed 1 tsp. vanilla 1 tsp. sea salt	Combine all ingredients in a food processor and process until desired consistency. Add a little bit of water if you need to. Once mixed well, scoop out dough and make a "patty" with your hands, about 1 square inch in size. Place on cookie sheet and bake at 375 degrees Fahrenheit for 15–18 minutes. (Or don't!) Remove and enjoy.

Four Weeks of Fabulous Food

"I've been vegan for 15 years, and it turns out it makes a very big impact on the environment to eat fewer animal products, which cause more greenhouse gases than all of transportation combined. The United Nations did a study just over two years ago, and that blew my mind. I started thinking that if people are vegetarian for just one day a week, that makes a huge difference!"[14]
—Emily Deschanel, actor

A wise man once told me to "eat to live, don't live to eat." (My grandpa.) But he obviously wasn't into eating as much as I was. He *clearly* underestimated my love for food.

In order to give you *zero* excuses for why you cannot begin to eat great food immediately, I've decided to make this process super easy for you. Welcome to four weekly menus of delicious vegetarian comfort foods. The menus are designed so that the foods that fall on weekdays are easy to bring to work, and the recipes that are a little more challenging or need to be hot are reserved for weekends. Also, I am a huge believer in not wasting food, so if the recipe serves four people, then I will probably list it again on the following day as a leftover. Waste not, want not, right?

If the meal plans include foods that you know make your life hell, then please substitute. For example, if you suffer from acid reflux and can't eat an orange, then eat an apple instead. If one of the recipes contains gluten, then please feel free to substitute for a gluten-free variety.

Keep in mind that one of the most difficult transitions that people make while overhauling their diet like this is to go from buying pre-packaged food to preparing everything themselves. It's a learning curve, but you can do it—and eventually will grow to love it. There's something special about making all of your own food, and it's a skill that your children and grandchildren will learn from you and thank you for. Let's get back to basics, shall we?

Week One Menu

Monday
Breakfast: Blonde Muesli (page 192).
Lunch: Spinach & Strawberry Salad
    (page 137).
Snack: Raw broccoli and carrot sticks
    with Holy Hummus (page 102).
Dinner: Green Spaghetti
    (page 141).

Tuesday
Breakfast: All Hail King Kale
    Smoothie (page 52).
Lunch: Waldorf(ish) Salad with
    ½ cup chickpeas (page 130).
Snack: 3 Coconut Bliss Balls
    (page 190).
Dinner: Easy as (Pizza) Pie
    (page 148).

Wednesday
Breakfast: Fresh Fruit Salad with Mint
    (page 85).
Lunch: 2 Nori Rolls (page 105).
Snack: Banana with ¼ cup walnuts.
Dinner: Seeds & Stuff Salad
    (page 135).

Thursday
Breakfast: #LifeIsPeachy Pudding
    (page 75).
Lunch: Superhero Salad (page 126).
Snack: 3 Coconut Bliss Balls
    (leftover).

Dinner: Lentil Loaf (page 155),
    Mazin' Mashed Potatoes
    (page 111), Wild Carrots
    (page 109).

Friday
Breakfast: Superhero Smoothie
    (page 54).
Lunch: Blistered Tomatoes
    (page 113).
Snack: Raw broccoli and carrot sticks
    with Holy Hummus (page 102).
6pm: Lazy Cabbage Roll Casserole
    (page 149).

Saturday
Breakfast: Banana-Walnut Pancakes
    (page 74).
Lunch: Tangy Lentil Salad
    (page 132).
Snack: Chocolate Chia Pudding
    (page 185).
Dinner: Green Salad with Tofu
    (page 134).

Sunday
Breakfast: Breakfast Rancheros
    (page 80).
Lunch: Steamed Green Salad
    (page 116).
Snack: 1 cup steamed organic
    soybeans with sea salt.
Dinner: Marie's Thai Curry
    (page 145).

Week Two Menu

Monday
Breakfast: Breakfast Quinoa
 with Honey and Bananas
 (page 76).
Lunch: Sesame Citrus Salad
 (page 127).
Snack: Apricot Bar (page 186).
Dinner: Squashed Puttanesca
 (page 152).

Tuesday
Breakfast: Tropicana Smoothie
 (page 52).
Lunch: Seeds & Stuff Salad
 (page 135).
Snack: 1 apple with 1 tbsp. almond
 butter.
Dinner: Stuffed Portabella
 Mushrooms (page 118).

Wednesday
Breakfast: Blonde Muesli
 (page 73).
Lunch: Garbanzo Quinoa Salad
 (page 125).
Snack: ½ cucumber with Holy
 Hummus (page 102).
Dinner: Rainbow Chard & Beet Salad
 (page 129).

Thursday
Breakfast: "Om" Oatmeal (page 81).
Lunch: Waldorf(ish) Salad (page 130).
Snack: Apricot Bar (leftover).
Dinner: Black Bean Tacos with Slaw
 (page 142).

Friday
Breakfast: Strawberry-Banana
 Smoothie (page 51).
Lunch: Superhero Salad (page 126).
Snack: 1 pear.
Dinner: Eggplant Lasagne (page 143).

Saturday
Breakfast: Denver "Eggs" (page 78)
 and 1 orange.
Lunch: Eggplant Pizza Rounds
 (page 97).
Snack: Kale Chips (page 96).
Dinner: Yam Burger (page 146).

Sunday
Breakfast: Banana-Walnut Pancakes
 (page 74).
Lunch: Grilled Bean & Green
 Quesadilla (page 154).
Snack: Apricot Bar (leftover).
Dinner: Red Lentil Soup (page 151).

Week Three Menu

Monday
Breakfast: Fresh Fruit Salad with Mint (page 85).
Lunch: Red Lentil Soup (leftover).
Snack: Raw broccoli and carrots sticks with Holy Hummus (page 102).
Dinner: Spinach & Strawberry Salad (page 137).

Tuesday
Breakfast: Rockin' Raspberry Smoothie (page 52).
Lunch: Waldorf(ish) salad with ½ cup chickpeas (page 130).
Snack: Chocolate Chia Pudding (page 185).
Dinner: Green Spaghetti (page 141).

Wednesday
Breakfast: Blonde Muesli (page 73).
Lunch: 2 Nori Rolls (page 105).
Snack: ½ an avocado filled with Fresh Salsa (page 94).
Dinner: Rainbow Chard & Beet Salad (page 129).

Thursday
Breakfast: #LifeIsPeachy Pudding (page 75).
Lunch: Superhero Salad (page 126).
Snack: 1 apple with 1 tbsp. almond butter.

Dinner: Sweet & Sour Tofu Stir-Fry (page 157).

Friday
Breakfast: Chunky Monkey Smoothie (page 54).
Lunch: Garbanzo Quinoa Salad (page 125).
Snack: 3 Coconut Bliss Balls (new batch—page 188).
Dinner: Lentil Loaf (page 155), Mazin' Mashed Potatoes (page 111), Wild Carrots (page 109).

Saturday
Breakfast: ½ cup Homemade Granola (page 83) with 1 cup unsweetened almond milk.
Lunch: Garbanzo Quinoa Salad (leftover).
Snack: Eggplant Pizza Rounds (page 97).
Dinner: Squashed Puttanesca (page 152).

Sunday
Breakfast: Breakfast Rancheros (page 80).
Lunch: 2 Stuffed Portabella Mushrooms (page 118).
Snack: 3 Coconut Bliss Balls (leftover).
Dinner: Eastern Lettuce Wraps (page 159).

Week Four Menu

Monday
Breakfast: "Om" Oatmeal
(page 81).
Lunch: Spinach & Strawberry Salad
(page 137).
Snack: Raw broccoli and carrot sticks
with Holy Hummus (page 102).
Dinner: Sesame Citrus Salad
(page 127).

Tuesday
Breakfast: Superhero Smoothie
(page 54).
Lunch: Seeds & Stuff Salad
(page 135).
Snack: 1 pear.
Dinner: Vegalicious Chili (page 160).

Wednesday
Breakfast: Fresh Fruit Salad with Mint
(page 85).
Lunch: Vegalicious Chili (leftover).
Snack: 3 Coconut Bliss Balls
(leftover).
Dinner: Green Salad with Tofu
(page 134).

Thursday
Breakfast: Breakfast Quinoa with
Honey and Bananas (page 76).
Lunch: 2 Nori Rolls (page 105).

Snack: ½ avocado filled with Fresh
Salsa (page 94).
Dinner: Rainbow Chard & Beet Salad
(page 129).

Friday
Breakfast: Protein Blast Smoothie
(page 52).
Lunch: Tangy Lentil Salad
(page 132).
Snack: Apricot Bar (page 186).
Dinner: Eastern Lettuce Wraps
(page 159).

Saturday
Breakfast: Banana-Walnut Pancakes
(page 74).
Lunch: Waldorf(ish) Salad
(page 130).
Snack: 1 cup steamed organic
soybeans with sea salt.
Dinner: Yam Burger (page 146).

Sunday
Breakfast: Denver "Eggs" (page 78)
and 2 slices of cantaloupe.
Lunch: Black Bean Tacos with Slaw
(page 142).
Snack: Apricot Bar (leftover).
Dinner: Eggplant Lasagne
(page 143).

Recipe Index

Endnotes

1 "Jamie Oliver: 12 Quotes From The Celebrity Chef You Won't Read in This Week's Cover Story." *LAWeekly Blogs*. 2011. Web. http://www.laweekly.com/squidink/archives/2011/06/20/jamie-oliver-12-quotes-from-the-celebrity-chef-you-wont-read-in-this-weeks-cover-story

2 Diaz, Cameron with Sandra Bark. *The Body Book*. New York: Harper Collins, 2014, p. 17.

3 http://www.globalhealing-center.com/natural-health/quotes-about-health/

4 Knight, Peter. "The Road to Health is Paved with Good Intestines." *Apothecary by Design*. 2012. Web. http://www.apothecarybydesign.com/blog/archives/173

5 "The Buddha On Nutrition: Every Human Being Is the Author of His Own Health or Disease." *Art of Dharma*. 2011. Web. http://www.artofdharma.com/every-human-being-is-the-author-of-his-own-health-or-disease/

6 "Quotes: Gary Hopkins." *QuotesGem*. 2014. Web. http://quotesgem.com/author/gary—hopkins

7 Pollan, Michael. *Food Rules*. New York: Penguin, 2009, p. 1.

8 *FamousVeggie.com 2014. Web.* http://www.famousveggie.com/quotes.aspx

9 "Ellen Page - Eating Healthy on the Go" *YouTube* 2014. Web. http://www.youtube.com/watch?v=vqnUQsoaG3Q&feature=youtu.be

10 "The 50 Best Quotes About Health & Nutrition." *Global Healing Center*. 2011. Web. http://www.global-healingcenter.com/natural-health/quotes-about-health/

11 "The 50 Best Quotes About Health & Nutrition." *Global Healing Center*. 2011. Web. http://www.global-healingcenter.com/natural-health/quotes-about-health/

12 "The 50 Best Quotes About Health & Nutrition." *Global Healing Center*. 2011. Web. http://www.global-healingcenter.com/natural-health/quotes-about-health/

13 "Doctors Prescribe Plant-Based Diets for Heart Disease." *Care2*. 2014. Web. http://www.care2.com/greenliving/doctors-prescribe-plant-based-diets-for-heart-disease.html

14 FamousVeggie.com 2014. Web. http://www.famousveggie.com/quotes.aspx

ABOUT THE AUTHOR

JENNIFER BROWNE completed her Bachelor of Arts Degree in English Literature at the University of the Fraser Valley, and has a Certificate in Plant-Based Nutrition from the T. Colin Campbell Center for Nutrition Studies. Although diagnosed with IBS in 2001, she has been symptom-free since the fall of 2010, which coincides with her adoption of a plant-based diet. Jennifer is an advocate for nutrition education, an award-winning member of the National Association of Nutrition Professionals (NANP), and a volunteer for Earthsave Canada. She freelances for a variety of health and wellness publications, and lives with her husband and three children just outside of Vancouver, British Columbia.

Visit her website at www.jenniferbrowne.org, explore her Facebook page at facebook.com/happyhealthylife.org, and find her on Twitter @jennifer_browne.